THE HEART IN

Christopher Bryant SSJE

THE HEART
IN PILGRIMAGE

*Christian Guidelines for the Human
Journey*

Darton, Longman and Todd
London

First published in Great Britain in 1980
by Darton, Longman and Todd Ltd
89 Lillie Road, London SW6 1UD

© 1980 Christopher Bryant SSJE

ISBN 0 232 51458 5

Printed in Great Britain by The Anchor Press Ltd
and bound by Wm. Brendon & Son Ltd,
both of Tiptree, Essex

CONTENTS

PRAYER

Prayer, the Church's banquet, angels' age,
    God's breath in man returning to his birth,
    The soul in paraphrase, heart in pilgrimage,
The Christian plummet, sounding heaven and earth;

Engine against the Almighty, sinner's tower,
    Reversèd thunder, Christ-side-piercing spear,
    The six-days'-world transposing in an hour,
A kind of tune, which all things hear and fear;

Softness, and peace, and joy, and love, and bliss,
    Exalted manna, gladness of the best,
    Heaven in ordinary, man well drest,
The Milky Way, the bird of Paradise;

Church bells beyond the stars heard, the soul's blood,
The land of spices, something understood.

GEORGE HERBERT

PREFACE

The Heart in Pilgrimage is a sequel to my two earlier books, *Depth Psychology and Religious Belief*[1] and *The River Within*[2]. Why have I written a third book? Indeed, why have I written at all on a subject which has been written about so often? It is partly the desire to share with my fellow pilgrims on the human journey some of the insights which I have gained from my own experience, from my ministry to others and from others' ministry to me, from reading and study and from prolonged reflection upon it all. But it is also the desire to explore those insights further by trying to express them in words. For the wrestling with words and meanings, the raids on the inarticulate, extend the understanding's grasp of realities which elude it. *The Heart in Pilgrimage* traverses the same territory as the other two books but with a different purpose. The earlier books tried to demonstrate that psychology can both illuminate Christian faith and life and show its contemporary relevance. They both had in mind readers who were outside or only on the fringe of the Christian community. In the present book the importance of psychology for Christian living is taken for granted. Though it also has in mind readers who would not call themselves Christians, it is aimed primarily at Christian readers who wish to strengthen their commitment and those who have responsibility for helping them in this endeavour.

Inevitably there has been some repetition of what was written in the earlier books, but I have tried to reduce this to a minimum and to treat in a different manner matters which were too important to

[1] Mirfield Publications 1972.
[2] Darton, Longman and Todd 1978.

ix

be omitted. In *The River Within* no less than four chapters were devoted to the theory and practice of prayer. For this reason less has been said about method and technique in prayer than might otherwise have been expected. But, if prayer be understood in the broad sense of a turning of the heart and mind to God which orients and pervasively influences the whole of life, then *The Heart in Pilgrimage* is concerned about prayer all the time. The image of a pilgrimage, a journey to some holy place, is taken as the symbol of a gradual and growing orientation of the heart to God, of a process in which a person ever more completely centres himself upon the holy of holies where God indwells him.

To write about the human journey as I understand it is to move between two mysteries, the lesser mystery of man and the greater mystery of God. The writer's task is to try to bring some light and clarity into these opaque realities without abolishing their mysteriousness, their unfathomable depths. He must seek to discover and map paths in the dense forest so that those who venture into it will not lose their way. He needs to take especial care to resist the prevalent positivist and reductionist spirit which aims at describing reality in clear, easily understood terms, ignoring or explaining away the penumbra of mystery that surrounds all real objects. The most powerful ally in resisting the debunking spirit of modern reductionism is poetry. For poetry opens the magic casements of the mind to a vision of reality which it perceives and rejoices in but cannot, except very imperfectly, comprehend. The symbols of poetry awaken wonder, they startle the mind and imagination into sensing facts and truths which leaden-footed logic could never have discovered.

In this book I have entered into dialogue with one poem of George Herbert, who has some claim to be considered the greatest religious poet in the English language. My hope is that it will save me, who likes writing to be clear, from reducing high mystery to the level of humdrum common sense. The chapter headings drawn from the poem do not wholly fit the contents of the chapters. How could they? I hope that they will stimulate the imagination of the reader to grasp more than my pedestrian prose can express. I was unable to find any phrase from the poem which would even approximately fit the subject of Chapter eight. Accordingly I have chosen a phrase from another of Herbert's poems, that on the twenty-third psalm.

I have to thank Miss Lesley Riddle of Darton, Longman and Todd for her encouragement and criticism. I am indebted to Mrs Wendy Robinson for encouraging me to make use of George Herbert's poem and to the comments of several members of my community who have read the first draft in whole or in part. I am grateful to my friend Terence Miller for contributing the cover design of the book as he did of *The River Within*.

OXFORD, JULY 1979   CHRISTOPHER BRYANT SSJE

The Land of Spices:
THE HEART'S JOURNEY

1

The phrase the land of spices, with its hints of hazardous adventure with some Columbus in search of the Spice Islands or of an El Dorado across the Atlantic, is, of course, an image of heaven, the hoped-for goal of man's pilgrimage. George Herbert's poem surprises us by announcing that prayer, here and now, admits us into this haven of the blest, it is a foretaste of the life of the angels, it is 'softness, and peace, and joy, and love, and bliss'. It is a beginning in the conditions of time of the joyous rhythms of eternity. But it is only a beginning. There is much in this life, as Herbert well knew, which is far from heavenly. To reach the land of spices, whose shores we touch in prayer, is to undertake a long and strenuous journey; it will involve our growing upwards and downwards like a tree, which is able to stretch out its branches to the sky only because it also sends down roots into the nourishing earth. The journey to the land of heart's desire is a highly personal journey demanding deliberate choices and decisions. We shall never arrive at journey's end by just drifting, whether alone or in company with others. But the journey is made with our fellows whose help we need and who equally need our help. We need one another's help partly because we are all subject to sicknesses of the soul. Sometimes we may need expert help, at other times we need the encouragement of companions who share our aims and are going our way. The help we get from others is useful in so far as it enables us to help ourselves, for in the last resort no one can solve our problems for us. Nothing and no one can relieve us of the responsibility of choosing and following our own path.

The land of spices can be understood as salvation, which includes complete wholeness and health; and as we step out towards this goal we can expect to share increasingly in its wholeness. But we cannot say that holiness always makes for health under the conditions of earth; there are too many examples of chronic invalids who radiate love and spiritual joy to make this equation plausible. At the same time we cannot treat physical health as a matter of indifference, for soul and body form a psycho-physical unity and an unhealthy body may affect the health of the soul. The opposite truth that sickness of soul affects the health of the body has become recognised increasingly in modern medicine, which sees a psychosomatic factor in many illnesses. It is widely known that anger which a person feels but is unable to express sometimes gives rise to migraine or acute depression, and continuous over-anxiety may cause peptic ulcers.

Both health and salvation can be understood as harmonious relationships – within our own psycho-physical being, with our fellows and, undergirding both, with God. These relationships interpenetrate one another. Salvation, though it means primarily a right relationship with God, must embrace the other two. For this reason it is inconceivable except within a transfigured society, such as we cannot imagine in this world. The human pilgrim sets out in search of the city of God, the land of spices, a country beyond the rim of the sky, though he may not realise that this is what he at bottom desires. Indeed he may believe that this hope is illusory. In this book I take for granted the general truth of the Christian belief in the world to come without attempting to set out the grounds for this belief. But the hope of life to come in no way absolves us from the task of making this world a better place. The person who sincerely prays 'Thy Kingdom come, thy will be done on earth as it is in in heaven,' is committed to seeking some foretaste at least of heaven in this world and to working to make this earth some approximation to the Kingdom, to a society where justice and love rule. Coming events cast their shadows before them and heavenly salvation should be foreshadowed here in health, peace and holiness, or at least in some incipient signs of these blessings.

The human pilgrimage involves struggle, for although man is born with immortal longings he is also born into a world partly estranged from its Maker. The myth of the fall of man and his expulsion from Eden expresses in story form certain timeless truths about man: that he has been created by God and is therefore fundamentally good, but that he fails to correspond with God's purpose and so finds himself in the grip of an evil in his own being and in society around him, which constantly frustrates his deepest needs. He finds himself unable to follow the road to salvation, to the City, to the 'Country far beyond the stars', where alone he can realise himself to the full. But the story of the fall is completed by the story of God's love and mercy working to undo its effects and bring good out of evil. This loving-kindness of God, uniquely displayed in the life, death and resurrection of Jesus Christ, is present and at work everywhere. It presses and persuades men towards the fulfilment especially of three basic needs of man: the need to realise and live out his humanity to the full, the need to love and be loved by his fellows and, penetrating and completing these other needs, the need to be at one with God.

Let us look more closely at the nature of health and wholeness. Because it consists in relationships which are all the time changing, health must be understood dynamically as a kind of graceful strength which adjusts itself to always changing circumstances. Milton's description of Eve in the Garden of Eden suggests something of this dynamic character of human wholeness: 'Grace was in all her steps, heaven in her eye,/ In every gesture dignity and love.' Milton's picture is an ideal one of unfallen woman. There is a rhythm, an ever-shifting balance in health to which we approximate more or less closely. But the recollection of Eden reminds us that we are not now in Paradise and that we have ceaselessly to contend with forces hostile to health. The forces are both outside and within. We are under the influence of a society which is sick. We cannot do without society, for it is only through relationships with others that our humanity develops. Nor is society by any means wholly bad. But it tends to exalt material wealth and prosperity above more truly human values, and to bring pressure to bear on individuals to conform to its ways and pursue its less than human goals. But the individual finds himself on the defensive not only against social pressures but also against tendencies within himself. In the course of growing up he learns to suppress feelings and impulses which clash with the expectations of parents and teachers. It is possible that the state called 'original sin' which used to be thought of as genetically transmitted is predominantly due to social inheritance, to the moulding influence of a sick society upon those who are born and grow up within it.

Original sin, the tendency to follow the worse despite perceiving the better, to evade burdensome duty, to subordinate the good of others to our own personal aggrandisement, to put animal ecstasy above spiritual fulfilment, can be understood in part as the failure of *homo sapiens* to manage his inheritance of animal instinct. The life of animals, ruled as it is by instinct, has a simplicity which human life lacks. Man has a power to think and reason and pursue goals which are far removed from the primary ends of animal instinct, to get the food necessary for survival, to avoid predators and to preserve the species by mating and caring for the young. These instincts though alive and strong in man do not determine his life as they do that of his animal cousins. Man has a freedom to pursue goals which are only tenuously linked with biological instinct. It is as though man is able to divert some of the stream of psychic energy, which in animals flows almost exclusively along the bed of biological instinct, into the channels of art, of culture and of religion. Our humanity drives us to make this diversion of energy, but we are forced to pay a price in the loss of the animal innocence of a creature whose actions are predetermined by instinct and in the taking up of the burden of responsibility and moral choice. We cannot avoid the painful dilemma of having to choose between competing loyalties or between duty and desire. 'Man was made for joy and woe,' sang William Blake, and much human frustration and sickness are results of the attempt to evade pain which should have been faced and endured. In childhood we usually experience some of the animal innocence, the freedom to act with a spontaneity, a carefree zest, which has not been 'sicklied o'er with the pale cast of thought'. Sometimes in retrospect childhood seems like the Garden of Eden. But this is largely illusory, for childhood has its bitter woes, which we tend to forget, as well as its ecstatic joys which we remember. There is no way back to Eden, the only road leads on.

2

The road which leads to man's fulfilment is one that brings him to an ever-closer oneness with God, his author. But God's presence, unseen and unknown, is with him from the beginning. The Christian theologian understands him as both transcendent over the universe and immanent within it. He sees him within each item of creation from the largest of the giant stars to the smallest of the sub-atomic particles. He is an inexhaustible power for good and an inexhaustible fund of invention and contrivance, causing everything to exist and, further, persuading the myriads of units competing for elbow room into patterns and wholes, thus creating relative harmony out of apparent mindless chaos. G. K. Chesterton has expressed in a poem the immanence of God in nature:

Elder father, though thine eyes
Shine with hoary mysteries,
Can'st thou tell what in the heart
Of a cowslip blossom lies?

Smaller than all things that be,
Secret as the deepest sea,
Stands a little house of seeds
Like an elfin's granary.

Speller of the stones and weeds,
Skilled in nature's crafts and creeds,
Tell me what is in the heart
Of the smallest of the seeds.

God Almighty, and with him
Cherubim and Seraphim
Filling all eternity,
Adonai, Elohim.[1]

The language of poetry and metaphor is better able to open the windows of the mind to some understanding of divine mystery than that of exact statement. The function of the latter is rather to exclude some of the extravagancies of unbridled imagination and to bring some order out of the profusion of metaphor and simile. As inheritors of the Hebrew Scriptures which are permeated with the sense of the living God whose Word is active throughout creation,

[1] 'The Holy of Holies', *The Collected Poems of G. K. Chesterton*, Methuen 1950.

we understand God's presence dynamically, as action. To picture his presence in the depth of created things suggests his action from within gently pressing and persuading each unit to fulfil its potential, to be itself so far as the presence of other units makes this possible. God is to be understood as moving the creatures not as an external force from without, but as a sustaining strength from within. It is part of the Christian spiritual tradition that God dwells in the centre of every man, an unseen, largely unknown Strength and Wisdom, moving him to be human, to grow and to expand his humanity to the utmost of its capacity. This divine indwelling is sometimes pictured as an inner sanctuary, an inviolable holy of holies within the house of the soul, sometimes as a fastness inaccessible to any save God alone:

> The hold that falls not when the town is got,
> The heart's heart whose immurèd plot
> Hath keys thyself keep not.
>
> Its keys are at the cincture hung of God,
> Its doors are trepidant to his nod,
> By him its floors are trod.[2]

It is because a person is able in prayer to find God in this inner sanctuary that even on this earth he can touch the shores of the land of spices; and 'the softness, and peace, and love, and joy, and bliss', which on rare occasions he feels are signs which assure him of God's presence within.

St Teresa of Avila, in her *Interior Castle*[3] has pictured the soul as a great palace containing many rooms. Spiritual progress advances as a person in response to the divine invitation is led step by step to the central room of the palace where God dwells. St Teresa understands this inner movement as an increasingly intimate experience of God and a growing conformity to his will. In her writings, which were mainly designed to give instruction in interior prayer to nuns, she describes states of prayer in which more and more of the soul's energies are concentrated on God. But although the saint

[2] From 'A Fallen Yew', Francis Thompson, *Poems*. Vol 1. Burns & Oates.
[3] There is an edition of the *Works of St Teresa*, edited and translated by Professor Allison Peers in three volumes. 'The Interior Castle', is in Vol II, Sheed and Ward 1946.

uses the degree of a person's concentration in prayer as one measure of his progress, she insists that, if genuine, the prayer will change a person's relationships with his fellows and his attitude to the demands of life. She was well aware of the possibility of illusion where a person's inner experience is looked upon as the criterion of his conformity to God. She is emphatic that the only sure test of oneness with God is growth in love and humility.

It is not uncommon for a person quite early in life to become aware of God as a presence within or around him. Sometimes this experience comes in childhood, more often in adolescence. Whether or not the experience is likely to grow or to fade depends on how seriously he takes it. Brother Lawrence in his *The Practice of the Presence of God*[4] has described his first overwhelming experience of God as he was contemplating a tree bare of leaves in the winter. That awareness never left him because by entering a monastery he took steps to make the experience the guiding star of his life. In his *Memories, Dreams and Reflections* the psychologist, Carl Jung, recalled in his old age that at the age of fifteen, 'Nobody could rid me of the conviction that it was enjoined upon me to do what God wanted not what I wanted. That gave me strength to go my own way. Often I had the feeling that in all decisive matters I was no longer among men, but was alone with God.'[5] This awareness of God remained an important and determining factor throughout his life and enabled him to make his unique contribution to the psychology of religion.

There is an enormous variety of human beings, all of them created by God and all of them invited to find their fulfilment in a relationship with him. Those who early in life become aware of God and make the search for closer union with him the major aim of their life have a special importance for their fellows as signs pointing to the true goal of everyone. The fourteenth-century spiritual writer, Walter Hilton,[6] describes this search under the simile of a pilgrimage to Jerusalem. Hilton tells the pilgrim to ignore or resist everything that might distract him from this object. He warns him of the difficulties of the journey, of the thieves who will waylay him and seek to rob him, of the seeming friends who will entice him to take

[4] Paperback edition, Burns & Oates 1977.
[5] Fontana 1967.
[6] *The Ladder of Perfection*, translated by Leo Shirley-Price, Penguin 1953.

his ease and enjoy himself. But he promises that if despite all that befalls him he perseveres, he will infallibly reach his journey's end in safety. He is to carry in his head and heart and repeat to himself constantly on the way such words as 'I am nothing, I have nothing, I desire nothing but the love of Jesus and to be with Jesus in Jerusalem.' Walter Hilton writes for those called to the contemplative life, the highly specialised life of a tiny minority of men and women. This life requires the renunciation of many human goods in order that a person's whole energy may be concentrated in responding to God's summons to a close and consciously realised union with himself. But many who are not called to the sharp renunciations of the contemplative life are strongly drawn to seek an increasingly conscious union with God in the course of managing a home, working in a business or engaging in a profession. Charles Williams has written of two ways of spiritual life, the way of the negation of images and the way of the affirmation of images. Those on the one way seek God by renouncing much of the life of the senses and imagination, by turning away from the richness of the creation to the infinite richness of the Creator. Those on the other way find in the light and colour and beauty, in the music and the dance of the created world, a gateway into the divine presence. Actually no one can follow either way exclusively. Those who seek God in the silence and seclusion of their own hearts need some stimulus from nature or from human companionship to help their approach to God. Many are the stories of hermits who made friends with animals. Equally those who seek God primarily through relations with people or through religious ceremonies or through the beauty and grandeur of nature or art need the discipline of occasional times of silence and withdrawal.

3

The few for whom the awareness of God is a deeply significant fact in their lives are called to be a sign to the many of a spiritual reality which they might otherwise overlook or ignore. For the majority of people, it would seem, do not have any conscious awareness of God, except perhaps for fleeting moments which are quickly forgotten or dismissed as illusory. It is possible to indicate a number of causes contributing to this imperceptiveness: the influence of the prevailing outlook of a civilisation shaped by science and technology which subordinates non-material values to the over-riding concern to mantain and improve the standard of living; the reaction against oversimple anthropomorphic conceptions of God which seem totally inadequate in face of the mysterious universe; a revulsion against a narrow religious upbringing. But whatever the reasons why the name or the idea of God seems unreal and religion of no importance, no one escapes the pressure and the pull of the unseen Wisdom and Love which draws one towards wholeness and fulfilment. There are values which we cannot but want to uphold, values which though they can be conceived of as independent of God are in fact the ropes and pulleys by which God draws men and women to him. These values were summarised more than two thousand years ago as truth, goodness and beauty.

Concern for truth, for accurate thinking, for the correspondence of thought and thing, of idea and reality, is fundamentally congenial to the human mind. Love of truth is not only the possession of philosophers, scholars and scientists but of ordinary people without great intellectual attainments. The housewife and the farmer, the clerk and the mechanic, are concerned in their different ways for true and accurate knowledge. Men lie and evade the truth, sometimes for gain, sometimes for self-protection, but they do this as a rule reluctantly, sometimes shamefacedly, for other things being equal they would prefer to know and to speak the truth. Concern for truth is a silken chain by which the Creator draws men to seek him. Another of the lures by which the Omnipotence draws men to search for him is the attraction of goodness, especially moral goodness. Men and women who are conscious of many shortcomings and would not dream of considering themselves to be good feel the fascination of goodness in others. This instinct to pay honour where honour is due, to salute outstanding courage or generosity, is part of the very substance of human nature. Hypocrisy has been called the homage which vice pays to virtue. The fact that many people feel it necessary to pretend to be better than they are bears witness to man's ineradicable craving for goodness.

The third of this trio of values, which together have set eternity in man's heart and awakened longings which nothing in this world can finally assuage, is beauty. A puritan tradition which has strongly influenced Anglo-Saxon religious sensibility has made us suspicious of beauty. The suspicion derives in part from a manichean tendency to regard the body as evil, which though rejected in theory by the Christian who believes God to be the Author of the human body as of the whole material world, is none the less powerful at the level of sentiment and emotion. We need to return to the view of St Augustine who thought of God as the uncreated Beauty, ancient but always new, the Fountainhead of all created beauty. How sensitive to beauty a person is depends on upbringing as well as on inborn temperament. But almost everyone to some degree feels the charm of beautiful scenery or the beauty of the human face and form. Beautiful sights and sounds can stab us with a longing for the joy of a beauty that will last, for the soft breath of the land of spices, for the blissful vision of the uncreated Beauty.

The Christian believer rightly relates the concern for truth, goodness and beauty to the God in whom he believes. He sees in God supreme Truth, ultimate Reality, he sees in him the Goodness inspiring and supporting all human goodness, he sees the living Loveliness which every earthly thing of beauty salutes. The recognition of God as the Source of all human values should lead the believer to see that the honouring and upholding of these values is part of the service of his Maker, an essential element in right worship.

The believer should be deeply concerned for the truth of what he believes; faith and love of truth should walk hand in hand. Today the believer's commitment to truth can be arduous and painful. We did not invent or discover the faith; we received it in the first place on authority. St Augustine affirmed that he would never have believed had not the authority of the Church persuaded him. The Christian faith is the faith of a community of believers and we usually come to believe on the authority of that community or of some members of it. If this sounds shocking to some who think it each person's duty to construct his own faith, it should be remembered that practically all knowledge is received on authority in the first place, and in many spheres of knowledge most people never question what the experts tell them. 'Only physicists really know the truth of physics,' wrote W. G. Pollard, the American physicist, 'everyone else has to take it on faith.'[7] Further a great deal of knowledge can be gained only by associating with those who have

[7]In *Physicist and Christian*, SPCK 1962; quoted by Alan Wilkinson in *Catholic Anglicans Today*, Darton, Longman and Todd 1968.

it. 'Both becoming a Christian and becoming a scientist involve
incorporation into a community, sharing its accumulated knowledge
and wisdom, growing into its outlook and venerating its saints.
Only when one has received a tremendous amount can one begin
to make an original contribution.'[8] In the contemporary world however, where only a minority of people adheres to the Christian faith,
questions are bound sooner or later to arise in the Christian's mind
as to the truth of his belief. Indeed, to reflect upon and to ask
questions about what has been received on authority, and to re-
examine it in the light of contemporary ideas and personal experience is the natural and properly human way of grasping truth and
making it our own. A vigorous faith must be constantly seeking
fuller understanding. None the less to confront seriously facts or
ideas which appear to throw doubt upon our previously held con-
victions can be extremely painful. I am tempted to evade the challenge, to look the other way, to silence the nagging doubt and refuse
to listen to it. Unfortunately, if I do this the question does not walk
away but burrows down into my unconscious, perhaps without my
realising the fact, and proceeds to eat away at my faith, robbing it
of its freshness and vitality. What needs to be done, to avoid the
petrifying of a faith which ought to be alive and growing, is to
cultivate what John Keats has called 'negative capability'. He has
described this attitude of mind as, 'when a man is capable of being
in uncertainties, mysteries, doubts, without any irritable reaching
after fact and reason'.[9] A kind of dialogue in the mind needs to be
encouraged between the old and the new until either the new is
rejected as wholly incompatible with the old or, as more often
happens, the old ideas are slightly modified in order to accommo-
date the new. Growth towards oneness with God, which also means
growth towards wholeness, means a growing openness to truth and
a growing determination to escape from ignorance and abandon
error wherever it is detected.

The journey towards oneness with God will mean also a growing
desire for goodness. A person will become increasingly determined
to act with courage and generosity, to serve the common good
wisely and energetically, to rejoice in the success or good fortune of
others. But whoever sets out resolutely for the country where love

[8] Op. cit.
[9] Letter to G. and T. Keats 1817.

and justice reign will inevitably be brought face to face with a disconcerting paradox, the failure to understand which will make his endeavours self-defeating. The more seriously he commits himself to the journey the more surely he will be forced to confront and come to terms with inner fears and desires, loves and hates, which seem to be in conflict with the whole aim and direction of the journey. He cannot get rid of these powerful urges and emotions however hard he tries. For one thing, his efforts will succeed only in repressing them so that they will operate against his intentions without his knowing it. More importantly, these inner energies are an essential part of him and in a transmuted form are needed if he is to complete his journey successfully. Real moral goodness is a gift to be received, a grace from God which must indeed be co-operated with but cannot be gained by effort alone. Further, the search for goodness to which God draws us is not the quest for a purely personal and private goodness, it is the search for the city of God where our fellows will be included equally with ourselves and for some foreshadowing of the city in the world of today. To be indifferent to the battle to build Jerusalem on the soil of this earth is to be only half committed to the Christian journey.

It has to be admitted that beauty has played a much smaller part than either truth or goodness in the Christian understanding of the Godward journey. Perhaps this is one reason for the joylessness of some Christian writing; for beauty makes for joy. It is true that it can awaken a greed to possess, a covetousness which can be so absorbing as to be fittingly termed idolatry. It is probably for this reason that many good men regard beauty with suspicion as a seducer from the pursuit of oneness with God, or at best as a relaxation from life's strains and stresses. But whatever grain of truth there may be in this conception of beauty as a danger and a distraction to man in his fallen condition, beauty must be accepted as something God-created and God-intended. The puritan revulsion from beauty, however understandable as a reaction against a pagan sensuality, has led to an impoverishment of human life. C. S. Lewis has written of the joy which beauty sometimes awakened in him as the guide eventually leading him to faith in God. For beauty awakens a joy, a delight, which summons us to the uncreated Beauty and the inexhaustible Fountain of joy. There is a bitter-sweet quality in the sights and sounds which woo our senses just because they point beyond themselves. They awaken longings which they are not meant to satisfy and so beckon us to the living God whose heralds they are. Unfortunately we try to grasp and prolong the moments of joy with which beauty blesses us. The search for God summons us to a certain detachment from the objects which delight us, to appreciate beauty without attempting to possess it or cling to it or the delight which beauty rouses. This restraint is helped by the realisation that detachment enriches and deepens appreciation.

He who binds to himself a joy
Doth the winged life destroy;
He who kisses a joy as it flies
Lives in eternity's sunrise.[10]

It would be good if Christians in their theology, their worship and their living could express a commitment to beauty. For beauty is a sign, an echo of the joy and bliss of the heavenly country; and the expense of time, money and creative skill in the making of beautiful music or the visual loveliness of architecture, sculpture and painting is no waste but part of the acknowledgement due from man to his Maker.

The attraction of truth, goodness and beauty is felt in different ways by different types of people. Let us consider this in relation to a widely accepted division of persons into the predominantly extravert and the predominantly introvert.[11] The extravert turns with a ready welcome to the world around him, to other people and to his surroundings. The introvert turns more readily to the inner world of his thoughts and feelings, and his inner reactions to people and circumstances. The distinction should not be pressed, for everyone has both introvert and extravert tendencies, it is a question of more or less. The extravert under the stress of disappointment or hostile criticism is driven to introspection, is thrown in on himself despite his predominantly extravert bent. Similarly people and events outside him compel the introvert to give his attention to them and turn away from his private inner world. The typical extravert and the typical introvert will both respond to the values of truth, goodness and beauty, but in different ways. The former will especially value

[10] William Blake. *Political Sketches*, 'Several Questions Answered', *Collected Poems*, Penguin 1977.
[11] See Appendix, in which prayer is discussed in relation to Jung's psychological types.

accurate knowledge of the people and happenings around him. Truth for him will tend to mean accurate information about people, places and events, about what can be observed; he will tend to be interested in statistics and he will seek the greatest possible objectivity and the elimination of the subjective. To the typical introvert this kind of truth is apt to seem somewhat shallow. Truth for him will be an inner vision of the meaning and interrelatedness of people and things. He will value inner truth, genuine self-knowledge and the correspondence of outer action with inner being, the living out of his own truth and the shunning of pretence and dissimulation. Goodness for the extravert will mean upright conduct, practical acts of justice and charity. He will be sensitive to the need for social justice, he will value public acts of generosity. He will judge a man by his deeds and will appreciate the proverb that the road to hell is paved with good intentions. The typical introvert will tend to see goodness as a matter of the motive and the will. The just man for him will be the man who loves justice whether or not he is in a position to serve the common good in any conspicuous way. The widow's mite for him will be worth more than the rich gifts of the wealthy. There will be a similar difference in the typical extravert and introvert responses to beauty. For the one the beauty of nature, of mountain and lake, of sunset and rushing stream, is something objective, something out there. For the other it will be a light and a joy in the mind of the beholder. It will inspire his imagination and enrich his memory.

It is clear that both the outward-looking and the inward-looking ways of appreciating and responding to the summons of truth, goodness and beauty are complementary, each needs the other. It is through the actual visible and tangible world around us that God draws us to look beyond this world. It is by winning the allegiance of the inner man, of the heart, it is by awakening immortal longings that God leads men to set out on the journey to the heavenly country. Only God's powerful summons, spoken in accents which he cannot shut out, will persuade a man to undertake a pilgrimage which will prove long and arduous and will require God's help for every step of the way. For the journey is an inner journey, a pilgrimage of the heart, and will necessitate the cleansing and reordering of regions of his being outside his knowledge and control. The seeds of the love of truth, goodness and beauty are innate in man, but their development is hindered by self-regarding fears which like weeds spring up with them and choke them. The heart, though it cannot shut out the voices of eternity, finds itself tied and bound by attachment to the things of time. We suffer from emotional wounds inflicted unintentionally in infancy and childhood and from the moulding influence of a sick society, as well as the consequences of our own follies and misdeeds. The heart has painfully to struggle free before it can with single aim choose and adhere to its true goal. It needs both healing and disinfection which only God can bring about and then only if we allow it.

4

The general name we give to this movement of turning to, of searching for God, is prayer. Commitment to truth, goodness and beauty I understand to be a kind of prayer, veiled and unconscious in those who do not recognise the authority of these values as flowing from God. For I now use prayer in the broadest sense to include not only formal prayer and worship whether private or corporate, not only informal prayer, meditation and contemplation, but a general orientation of heart and mind which gives colour and direction to the whole of life. Sometimes a person in distress going to some trusted counsellor is really praying; it is God's help he is seeking through a human intermediary. Sometimes a person delighting in a Beethoven symphony or a painting by Rembrandt, or one of Shakespeare's sonnets, may be praising his Creator.

We can discern at least two fundamental elements in prayer. First there is desire, there is a longing for what we know is beyond our reach, which we can gain only as a gift. Prayer gives voice to a need which only God can supply. It is easier to recognise the longing which prayer articulates than to state with any precision what it is that we long for. I suggest that there are at least three strands in it. First, there is a longing for wholeness, to be fully and completely ourselves, to be all of a piece, free from the desire to be or to appear other than what we are, to be totally spontaneous. This longing is part of the reason for the nostalgia for the imagined paradise of childhood. For the child with his spontaneity and unselfconscious naturalness is a symbol of qualities we long to possess. It is this longing for the wholeness, the all-of-a-piececess which we discern in some children which makes us respond to the poet's cry, 'Oh how I long to travel back/And tread again that ancient track.'[12] This longing for wholeness is closely joined to another longing, the longing to be at one with our fellows, the longing for a city of peace, a place where we would know and appreciate and love our fellows, and be known and loved in return. We are conscious of a need to disclose ourselves, which is balanced by the fear that to expose our real thoughts and feelings would make us vulnerable, would leave us open to ridicule or criticism. The peace of the city of our dreams is not the insipid peace purchased at the price of suppressing all opinions that might arouse controversy or disagreement. For the need to suppress strongly held views lest they disturb peace is due to a deficiency of mutual love and trust. Where the qualities of love and trust are strong, people are refreshed and stimulated by contrary points of view and feel themselves in no way threatened by them. The city for which we long is a place where the human qualities of each are recognised and rejoiced in by all. The third strand which includes without swallowing up the other two, is the desire for the Unknown, for the shoreless Sea, for God, for the vision of him in whom everything good and true and beautiful has its origin, who is the Fount of friendship, in whom there pulses an immense energy of giving and receiving, whose overflow is the created universe.

Prayer expresses a longing, vague and vast, for goods which pass our imagining. It also expresses faith. Desire perhaps normally implies some faith but it need not. Indeed, desire without any faith in the possibility of its fulfilment would be a description of hell; and this, alas, is one of the human options. But prayer not only expresses desire, it also voices faith. It is no cry in the empty darkness, it is addressed to a Presence and a Person. It involves commitment to a relationship which will carry a man out of his depths and lead him into situations which he does not and could not foresee. Prayer, undertaken seriously and confidently, launches a person on a journey; it brings about a transformation of his desires; it is a pilgrimage of the heart.

In this introductory chapter we have reflected on the nature and the hoped-for goal of the human journey. In the remaining chapters we shall explore more fully the meaning of the commitment in which faith involves us. In the second chapter we shall look more

---

[12] 'The Retreat', Henry Vaughan, *Collected Poems*, O.U.P. 1957.

closely at man's nature, rooted in the earth and aspiring to the skies. In the five following chapters we shall sketch the pilgrimage, its stages, scenery and landmarks, and the hazards and the discipline of the journey. Four matters of such importance in the pilgrimage as to require special treatment will then be dealt with in successive chapters. A final chapter will look back and try to gather up some bits and pieces which were left out and to tie up loose ends.

2

God's Breath in Man:

THE INDWELLING GODHEAD

1

In the previous chapter I referred both to the presence of God in the soul's centre and to the innate desire for union with God. It is necessary to look more closely at both these doctrines for they are fundamental to the Christian understanding of the human condition. We are not of course dealing with empirically observable and measurable fact but with metaphor and symbolic statement which is partly self-authenticating through its power to shed light on experience, partly accepted from its congruence with truths received on other grounds. For the Christian some of these other truths are those which relate to Jesus Christ in whom, so he believes, God has uniquely revealed himself. It is no part of the aim of this book to argue the truth of Christian belief but, while assuming its truth, to show how it illuminates and furthers the human quest.

The phrase, 'God's breath in man returning to his birth', which provides the heading for this chapter, awakens many echoes from the Bible. Two texts in particular spring to mind as shedding light on Herbert's meaning. The first is from the description of the creation of man in Genesis:'Then the Lord God formed man of dust from the ground, and breathed into his nostrils the breath of life; and man became a living being.'[1] The second is from St Paul's letter to the Romans: 'We do not know how to pray as we ought, but the Spirit himself intercedes for us with sighs too deep for words.'[2] Genuine prayer is a more than human activity. It is the

[1] Genesis 2.7.
[2] Romans 8.26.

Spirit of God within man breathing upon the divine spark, which is the innate desire for God, and fanning it into a flame of Godward aspiration. The desire for God resembles a fountain in the centre of our being which seeks to scatter its pure water over the heights and depths of the personality. Forces and influences of very different kinds block and partly nullify its healing and cleansing efficacy. The journey to the wholeness and abundant life of the city of God necessitates the overcoming and counteracting of these contrary pressures and pulls. But no effort or skill on our part can take the place of this inner fountain of desire. Indeed this deep thirst for God is part of what it means to be man. It is closely linked with the Spirit of God dwelling in us. Real prayer is God's prayer in us, it is the breath of God returning to his birth.

The opening chapter of Genesis describes the Spirit of God brooding over the dark waters of primeval chaos. It is a picture of God the Creator bringing order out of confusion and dispersing darkness by light. The same picture could illuminate the creation of man. The Genesis story pictures God as making clay out of the dust of the earth, shaping it into the form of a man, and then breathing into it the breath of life. Modern evolutionary science teaches us to see the shaping of man as the effect of hundreds of millions of years of evolution to produce man's animal parents. We can then picture the Creator Spirit brooding over the darkness of an animal living by obedience to its instinctive drives, breathing spiritual life into it and illuminating it with a dazzling light which discloses to it a new world of beauty, goodness and truth, and awakens it to an awareness of a Presence and a Majesty to which it owes its being. The Spirit of God in this picture not only illuminates the mind of man but brings order and unity into his unconscious depths, so that heart and mind are at one in single-hearted loyalty to his Author.

The picture I have sketched is an interpretation of the Genesis story in the light of our fuller knowledge of human origins. But the Genesis story itself is not to be understood as the account of an historical event. The inspired writer is telling his readers that the human nature which they saw exemplified all around them and experienced in their own persons is not what the Creator intends, it was not their real nature, it fell far short of God's original design. He did not think of it in this way; he thought of it in the way he wrote it, in terms of a story which would account for the condition of man in his estrangement from God, the story of Adam created perfect and at peace with his surroundings and with God, and through disobedience falling away from that original perfection and peace. Theologians later took this story to be historical and the fall through disobedience and the exclusion from Eden as actual facts which account for the defect in human nature, called original sin, which has been handed on to Adam's descendants. G. K. Chesterton spoke of the good news of original sin. He called it good news because it carried within it the implication that the selfish human nature with which we are familiar is not our real nature but a corruption of it, a lapse from it. But it is perhaps even better news if we understand our present condition not as the falling away from a perfection once attained and now lost, but as a halfway stage on a journey towards a perfection which lies ahead, to which the Creator is drawing us. Man then would be still in the making. The bliss of Eden is a dream of what could be, of what human nature at one with God might become. Following this interpretation, instead of the load of racial guilt which the old way of understanding the fall places on our shoulders, we should have a powerful incentive to work out our salvation, confident that the Creator having guided us thus far would continue to shepherd us along the road which leads, not back to Eden, but on to the Divine City. We get an idea of what human nature is meant to be not by looking back to the dream figure of Adam in Eden, but to another man, Jesus Christ. In that historical figure, sketched in the four gospels, we catch a glimpse of man as he is meant to be, as in essence he truly is, in so far as it could be disclosed in a short life, bounded by the limited horizons of first-century Palestine and caught up in the religious and political tensions of that time.

2

In the Genesis story man is described as being created in the image of God. 'So God created man in his own image, in the image of God he created him; male and female he created them.'[3] There is a certain affinity between man and his Maker, which has sometimes been referred to as a divine spark in man. There is a parallel to this biblical doctrine in the thinking of Carl Jung who finds the theo-

[3] Genesis 1.27.

logical idea of God's image in man akin to his own empirically
founded psychological concept of the Self. In his description of the
inner dynamics of men and women Jung uses the term archetype
to describe certain inherited quasi-instinctive tendencies. For example he calls the instinctive tendency of an infant to attach itself to
its mother, or to some mother surrogate, the mother archetype. The
image of the actual mother activates the mother archetype in the
child, and the archetype gives the image of the mother its power to
grip the imagination of the child. Indeed the image of the mother
can exercise such power that a boy or girl when growing up may
find it difficult to break away from its domination. Jung sees the
archetype of the Self as the most fundamental of these inherited
determinants, these instinctive tendencies. He uses the term to
indicate a shaping force within the personality which is universal
in its operation and which some people consciously experience.
What is experienced is the pressure upon the conscious personality
of an individual of heights and depths in himself of which he is
otherwise unconscious. Sometimes this is felt as the over-shadowing
influence upon a part exerted by the whole, sometimes as the mag-
netic pull of a centre within the depths of the personality. It is as
though the potential man is trying to become actual by inducing a
person to make the choices and decisions and to perform the actions
without which this actualisation cannot take place. This pressure
of the total Self seeking actualisation, though largely unconscious,
is immensely powerful. When it becomes conscious, as sometimes
in dreams, it is charged with absolute authority and is usually
surrounded by an atmosphere of the numinous. Jung sees this as
the root of the experience of God. The awareness of the inescapable
influence of the Self pressing a man to realise his potential to the
full is so much bound up with the experience of God that in practice
it cannot be distinguished from it. It is through responding to this
shaping force within the personality that a person becomes aware
of the Spirit of God within and behind him.

Psychology can neither prove nor disprove the truths of faith. But
it can help contemporary men and women, whether believers or
not, to take Christian doctrine seriously by shewing how closely
linked some of it is to empirical experience. It can also help the
believer in the practical task of responding to God's summons to
him to live out his humanity to the full. It can in particular bring
help to the many who, when they try to pray, feel that their efforts

are like a kind of make-believe, lacking reality and depth. One reason for this sense of superficiality is that their praying is too much a matter of conscious thinking and feeling and does not involve their depths, which may be totally out of harmony with what they consciously express. Dynamic psychology, which stresses the powerful influence that unconscious emotions, such as fear, anger, hate or love, exert on our conscious thoughts and actions, can shed much light on the inner obstacles to prayer and can enable us to turn what we had thought to be an enemy into an ally.

To make use of an illustration from an earlier book,[4] the conscious personality of an adult in relation to the inner world of the unconscious can be likened to the king of a country whose extent and population is very imperfectly known to him. It is his task to rule the country in the interests of the people as a whole, to maintain friendly relationships with neighbouring countries and to co-operate with them in promoting peace and order throughout the world. Among his people there are violent as well as peace-loving elements; there are aggressive and ambitious factions which from time to time attempt to take over the government of the country; there are gross and licentious groups which seek to win his favour and to lead him into lax and self-indulgent ways to the neglect of his task of government. His aim should be to get to know the diverse elements of his country, to listen with understanding and sympathy to their needs and concerns, but to stand up to them firmly and to rule. Some of his problems are inherited from a colonial period when his country was ruled by his parents and others who trained him for the day when he should become an independent ruler. During this period of tutelage he began his acquaintance with the people he was destined to rule, learning to make friends with some of them, coming to fear and dislike others. Some kings are much better equipped than others for ruling their country wisely. But there is one little understood but very important resource which, if discovered and relied upon, will enable the king gradually to exercise his authority over a loyal and co-operative people. In the heart of the kingdom there lies hidden a secret sanctuary where there lives a Spirit, wise and strong, who knows everything that is going on throughout the kingdom and will give to the king the wise guidance he needs, if

[4] Bryant, *Depth Psychology and Religious Belief*, Mirfield Publications 1972.

only he will seek him out and allow himself to be ruled by the Spirit's superior wisdom.

I use the illustration of a king and his kingdom to suggest something of the extent and complexity of our inner world which it is possible to overlook, despite the fact of its continuous influence upon us. Further, the hidden sanctuary where the Spirit dwells is no fancy touch but, as we have seen, a picture of what is not only the teaching of mystical writers but an experienced reality. Genuine prayer is always an utterance of the Spirit of God. Perhaps much that passes for prayer is not real prayer at all but the use of words without meaning them, or the expression of desire without faith. Real prayer is the breath of God returning to his birth. In prayer God speaks to God. The Spirit seeks to breathe life and a pure intention into every sincere effort to turn to God. It is the Holy Spirit in man who awakens him to the values of truth, goodness and beauty; it is he who awakens and directs the thirst which only union with God can satisfy; it is he who sets man upon the pilgrimage to the City of God where alone perfect wholeness and peace can be found. No man is without the indwelling presence of God, though most people are either ignorant of it or ignore it; and in everyone there are obstacles and counter-forces which hinder the Spirit's vivifying and liberating power.

3

The Christian however believes that through Jesus Christ the Spirit lives in him with special force and fire. Indeed the first Christians understood their empowering by the Holy Spirit as something altogether new. It is impossible of course to understand this as meaning that the Holy Spirit had not been present in the world and with man before the coming of Jesus Christ. There is however no difficulty here if we recall the doctrine of the Word set out in the prologue to St John's gospel.[5] There the gospel states that the Word was in the beginning with God, that all things were made through him, that he is the light of all men. All men have an inkling of the divine through the Word who illuminates man's spiritual understanding. The Word spoke through the Jewish prophets and is the

[5] John 1.1–14.

Author of whatever is true in all religions. Then the gospel goes on to say 'The Word was made flesh.' The Word spoke through a man with whom he was totally identified. Through the Word made man what the Word had spoken at other times and in other ways was clarified and made concrete. The newness of the coming of the Holy Spirit was like the newness of the coming of Jesus Christ. As in Jesus Christ the Word addressed mankind in a new and unexpected manner, so, as the result of the life, death and resurrection of Jesus, the Holy Spirit was enabled to indwell men and women in a fashion that took them by surprise. This indwelling by the Spirit was not totally new. It was the renewal of God's original purpose for man, it was the new clear statement of what had been true all along and had been dimly seen and partly expressed before.

If we are right to understand the coming of the Holy Spirit upon the disciples on the day of Pentecost as the crowning and completing of his action in the minds and hearts of prophets, seers and mystics of all times, places and religious cultures; if, that is, we stress the continuity of the work of redemption with that of creation and providence, nevertheless the release of the Spirit after Christ's resurrection seemed and was for the first disciples something new, unexpected and immensely powerful. This is how Charles Williams describes the descent of the Holy Spirit at Pentecost. 'At a particular moment, and by no means secretly, the heavenly Secrets opened upon them, and there was communicated to that group of Jews, in a rush of wind and a dazzle of tongued flames, the secret of the Paraclete in the Church. Our Lord Messiah had vanished in the flesh; our Lord the Spirit expressed himself towards the flesh and spirit of the disciples. The Church, itself one of the Secrets, began to be.'[6] That explosion of Spirit which occurred in a turbulent backwater of the Roman empire initiated a movement which, led by apostles and evangelists of whom the best known is St Paul, spread like wildfire through the cities which fringed the Mediterranean. Slowly but surely it captured the imagination of the Roman world, though not without many accommodations to pagan thought and ways. All through the history of the Church there has been a constant interaction and an interflow of ideas between it and its cultural environment. But at intervals throughout its history there have come times of spiritual renewal when Christians returned with

[6] *Descent of the Dove*, Chapter 1, Longman 1939.

redoubled attention to the rock whence they were hewn, the death and resurrection of Jesus the Messiah, and with that return to their origin there has come a fresh outpouring of the Holy Spirit.

One of the features of the ministry of Jesus which impressed his contemporaries and was recorded in all the four gospels was his healing of a great number of sick people and his liberation of men and women from demonic control. But these acts of healing and liberation, though seen as important signs of God's power and of the imminence of the Kingdom, were understood to be secondary to the new life of total loyalty to God, of openheartedness to others and an unlimited willingness to forgive injuries. That quality of living, though manifested in the life of Jesus himself, seems wholly beyond the capacity of ordinary flesh and blood. But with the coming of the Holy Spirit something of this quality of life began to shew itself in the first believers, who found themselves knit into a fellowship so intense as to make the sharing of possessions seem natural. The presence of the Holy Spirit brought many extraordinary spiritual powers to members of the Christian community, one of the most striking being the gift of healing the sick. The new quality of life among the disciples is described by St Paul when he writes of the fruit of the spirit being love, joy, peace etc. Some powerful metaphors are used in the New Testament to describe the change in those who had committed themselves to the Christian way by undergoing the rite of Baptism. Some of these metaphors are drawn from the symbolism of Baptism which in the first days of the Church was normally of adults and involved immersion in water. The newly initiated Christian had died to his old way of life and risen out of the baptismal waters into a new way. St Paul understood Baptism as an identification with the dying and rising again of the Messiah. He speaks of the Christian as in the Messiah and, though less frequently, of the Messiah as in the Christian. However we understand the spatial metaphor implied by the preposition 'in', it cannot mean less than a deep and penetrating influence of Christ upon the Christian. To be 'in Christ' is to be a new creation. St John's gospel speaks of new birth or birth from on high to describe the new relation to God which faith in Christ brings about; this faith implies a commitment which is expressed in Baptism and sealed by the Holy Spirit.

I have tried to draw out some of the meaning which the first Christians discovered in the life into which they were initiated when they received the Spirit. It was a shared life of brotherhood with their fellow-believers. No doubt there is some idealisation in the New Testament descriptions. The transformation in the new Christian's life was neither instantaneous nor complete. St Paul's exhortations to Christians to avoid such elementary sins as drunkenness, fornication and cruelty, and to walk worthy of their vocation makes this abundantly evident. There was undoubtedly much inconsistency between aim and achievement, between the ideal and the actual. But the great Pauline metaphors point to spiritual facts which were slowly moulding the lives of believers, to spiritual seeds which would come up and bear fruit if given the encouragement they needed. The Christian had the task of co-operating with something that had been given to him and done in him. This is expressed explicitly in the exhortation 'Work out your own salvation with fear and trembling; for God is at work in you.'[7] The Christian's inner life, his growth towards holiness, towards the living out of his humanity to the full, could be summed up as a co-operating with, a reliance upon, the Spirit of God, guiding, healing, liberating, warning him from within. In subsequent chapters we shall sketch in some detail a few of the ways in which we can co-operate with the Spirit and learn to rely on him. Here I want to outline briefly the nature and scope of this co-operating and in particular the initial turning to God, the change of attitude without which co-operation with the Spirit can hardly begin.

There are many persons who do not consciously seek oneness with God nor to be led or guided by the Spirit yet, nevertheless, appear to possess many of the characteristics of those who are wholly committed to the Christian way. Sometimes they are people who have been put off Christian belief by the inconsistencies of Christians, sometimes they have rejected some caricature of Christian doctrine, supposing it to be what Christians believe. But a person rejecting the Christian way or having never known it may unknowingly be led by the Spirit of God towards the same goal however differently he may conceive it. In this book however we shall be concerned with the road that Christians have followed and still follow, though in the twentieth century some of the old landmarks have disappeared and need to be replaced by new.

[7] Philippians 2.12–13.

4

Right at the outset of the Christian road a decision, accompanying a change of attitude, is made. The New Testament word which describes this change is *metanoia*. Though usually translated repentance it means literally change of mind or heart. It is sometimes called conversion and can be understood both passively, as something which happens to a person, and actively, as the decisions and actions which follow upon an inner change. It may be so sudden that a man can name the day and the hour when it occurred. In his poem, 'The Everlasting Mercy', Masefield described just such a sudden change in the life of Saul Kane, the drunkard and waster:

> I did not think, I did not strive,
> The deep peace burnt my me alive:
> The bolted door had broken in,
> I knew that I had done with sin.
> I knew that Christ had given me birth
> To brother all the souls on earth,
> And every bird and every beast
> Should share the crumbs broke at the feast.[8]

But more often conversion is a gradual process like the dawn of a summer day. Slowly the light grows until day has fully come, and it is impossible to point to a moment before which was night and after which is day. So a person often comes to realise that he is committed to the Christian way without being able to point to any one moment when the decision to follow Christ was made. But sudden conversion is never as instantaneous as it seems; slowly the waters rise and gather strength until at last the dam breaks. In 'The Everlasting Mercy' Masefield describes the rising of the waters as incident after incident brings home to Saul the folly and the wrongness of his life. The words which another Saul heard addressed to him, 'It is hard for you to kick against the goad', also point to an inner preparation for the sudden conversion which took place on the road to Damascus. There is an intellectual as well as an emotional factor in this change of direction and sometimes head and heart seem to be in opposition. C. S. Lewis tells us that he was

[8] *Collected Poems of John Masefield*, Heinemann 1946.

intellectually convinced of the truth of Christianity without any inner feeling of attraction towards it. Equally and more commonly a person may be attracted by the Christian story and by the character and teaching of Christ as described by the four evangelists without being able to give intellectual assent to the gospel.

How does this conversion come about? How do men and women come to believe and commit themselves to the following of Christ? The New Testament affirms that God himself brings this about, though he normally uses human agents. 'Faith comes from what is heard, and what is heard comes by the preaching of Christ.'[9] God speaks through those who proclaim the good news in Jesus, the Messiah, put to death by men but raised to immortal life to be an unseen presence with his disciples. One of the themes of St John's gospel is that of witness. Men are brought to see and recognise Jesus as Messiah through the testimony of others. Simon Peter is brought to Jesus by his brother Andrew, Nathaniel by his friend Philip. But there is a more powerful force at work than human testimony. Jesus, speaking to his disciples of their task after he has left them, says: 'When he the Counsellor comes, whom I shall send to you from the Father, even the Spirit of truth, who proceeds from the Father, he will bear witness to me; and you also are witnesses, because you have been with me from the beginning.'[10] The Holy Spirit is the primary witness; silently addressing the hearts and consciences of men and women he will persuade them of the truth; the witness of the disciples, important though it is, is secondary. God addresses men and women through a multitude of signs which focus their imagination and arrest their attention, so that they are unable to shut their ears to the voice of the Spirit within. The most potent of these signs are men and women wholly committed to God and his Kingdom. Unique among these is Jesus Christ, the Light of the world.

People are led to turn towards God and set out on the journey towards the City of God, the land of spices, when hope is awakened together with hope's sister, fear. In Jesus' story of the prodigal son it was hope that set the young man off on the journey home. No doubt the waking up to his miserable condition prepared him for the decision to go home, but his wretchedness would not have acted

[9] Romans 10.17.
[10] John 15.26–27.

as a spur if he had not had reason to hope that his father would receive him back. The gospel can speak to man's condition because it can lay bare his ineradicable desire to be at one with God through whom alone he is able to realise himself and grow to his full human stature. The gospel assures him that this desire of his heart can be satisfied, that his Creator will provide all the help he needs to reach journey's end. But he needs to be convinced of this. Before I am prepared voluntarily to undertake an arduous task I need to be satisfied not only that the work is worth doing but also that it is possible. The signs which will persuade me of this are the evidences which I see around me or hear about from those whose witness I trust, that the life of oneness with God is not impossible for me, that if I choose I can experience the love, joy and peace which flow from it. The atheist French lawyer, who out of curiosity paid a visit to the curé of Ars, at that time the talk of Paris, returned home a believer. When asked what had induced him to abandon his atheism he replied, 'I've seen God in a man.' No doubt it was some experience of this sort that drew disciples to Jesus; he made God real to them. St Luke records the impression he made on the rich tax-collector, Zacchaeus, whose profession and wealth proclaimed him as both grasping and unscrupulous. In the totally unlooked-for friendliness of Jesus in place of the contempt which he had expected, the presence and love of God came home to him overwhelmingly. He saw a new life stretching out before him and he decided to commit himself to it by a decisive act. 'Behold, Lord, the half of my goods I give to the poor; and if I have defrauded anyone of anything, I restore it fourfold.'[11] The Spirit of God moved him to act, the breath of God was returning to his birth.

A person's change of heart, his decision to give to God and his will the first place in his life, is a beginning only. The decision has to be implemented in day-to-day living. It is the setting out on a long, arduous but rewarding journey, which later chapters of this book will describe in detail. But demanding though the pilgrimage is, it is something to which our own nature presses us in order that we may find fulfilment. Earlier I alluded to certain determinants of human nature and in particular to what Jung has called the archetype of the Self, the instinctive tendency which presses men and women to seek wholeness, to live out their own truth, to activate to

[11] Luke 19.2–10.

the utmost of their capacity their human potential. The gospel crowns the insight of the psychologist by affirming that the Author of man's being has set eternity in his heart and summons him to complete in a life beyond the world the task begun here of discovering and living out his own truth. On the other hand, if faith in God can bring coherence to the discoveries of psychology and provide rational grounds for the human faith of the psychotherapist, psychology in its turn can help the believer in his spiritual journey. There is a mass of literature classifiable under the general heading of ascetic and mystical theology, which deals with the theoretical and practical aspects of the search for closer union with God. This literature seeks to apply the truths of the gospel as understood by the Church of their authors' time to the tasks, problems, joys and sorrows of the search for God. The authors of these writings naturally made use both of the psychology and of the proverbial wisdom of their day as well as of ideas inherited from their forefathers. Modern psychology can help us to discriminate between ideas and practices which were ephemeral and belonged to a culture long past, and those of perennial importance. It can also provide us with a set of words and ideas worked out by men wrestling with the human problems of our time and so can offer new and more effective tools for making known the reality and the power of the gospel.

Some of the old spiritual guides described three stages in the Christian journey and the practices appropriate to each stage. In the first of these stages, called the purgative way, the pilgrim's principal task is the struggle to confront and overcome the obstacles in himself, the old habits and attitudes, which hinder his journey. In the second stage, the illuminative way, progress is made chiefly through growing insight into the reality of God and the spiritual world in which the traveller is becoming increasingly at home. In the third stage, the unitive way, the pilgrim is concerned above all with God, with doing and accepting God's will. There are methods of prayer and self-discipline appropriate to each stage. The scheme should be understood flexibly, for the stages overlap. At the very outset of his journey the pilgrim is led on by the light of faith and seeks God and his will. To the very end he will be concerned to deepen his repentence and enlarge his faith. Further, individuals are led in many and differing ways according to temperament, early experience, present circumstance, and the call of God. Sometimes like a river which winds and loops and bends back on its course from its birth in the mountains to its goal in the sea, a person may travel by labyrinthine paths to reach the land of wholeness. But if these qualifications are borne in mind the threefold division of the Christian pilgrimage sheds light on the road. The next three chapters will roughly follow this ancient scheme, beginning with the purgative way in which the pilgrim especially confronts the grim reality of evil.

3

The Christian Plummet:

THE CONFRONTATION WITH EVIL

1

When a person seriously commits himself to the pilgrimage he is forced to face habits and tendencies in himself which run contrary to his commitment. During the first stage of the journey, tradition- ally called the way of purgation, the conflict with evil, the deliberate renunciation of what hinders the journey, must play a large part in a person's search for oneness with God. Saul Kane after his con- version decides to be a ploughman; he makes up his mind:

> That I should plough, and as I ploughed
> My Saviour Christ would sing aloud,
> And as I drove the clods apart
> Christ would be singing in my heart,
> Through rest-harrow and bitter roots,
> Through all my bad life's rotten fruits.[1]

The inspiration and vision which accompanied his conversion makes Saul feel that his new life will be simple and straightforward. But the old Saul has not been magicked away in the twinkling of an eye. It will live on for many a day and be a continual source of weariness and frustration. He rightly sees that the purgation of the old man must be the work of grace. But he will have to co-operate with grace if its cleansing and renewing work is to be well and truly accomplished. One of the tools of co-operation is a self-examination

[1] 'The Everlasting Mercy', *Collected Poems of John Masefield*, Heinemann 1946.

32

designed to deepen self-awareness, awareness of the underground desires and fears, the loves and hates, which are still alive and vigorous and, if unfaced, will render his new life precarious. Without this effort after self-awareness he will almost certainly fall into a smug and self-righteous attitude, as he reflects upon the contrast between what he once was and what he now is.

The search for self-knowledge is the indispensable task of the pilgrim throughout his journey but it is especially necessary in its early stages. Herbert's phrase, 'the Christian plummet sounding heaven and earth', part of which forms this chapter's title, hints at this search. It awakens the image of the leadsman standing in the ship's bows taking soundings with his plummet. The human journey is a perilous one and can lead to shipwreck on some hidden shoal. Prayer enables the pilgrim to discover the submerged sandbanks which might easily bring his voyage to grief. For prayer not only reaches up to heaven, but it also sounds the murky depths of our nature and the dark energies of earth. Indeed though heaven and earth are opposites it is only by confronting the reality of our earth-bound nature that we can safely reach out to the heavenly regions. In this chapter we shall consider this confrontation with evil which the quest for God necessitates. Before turning to the traditional teaching about this it will be useful to reflect on the subject in the light of modern psychology.

In both the previous chapters reference was made to the doctrine of original sin, which seeks to give some explanation of the fact that there is something wrong with men and women as they are. This defect can be understood as a defect of humanity, that is that we are insufficiently human. When *homo sapiens* separated himself from his pre-human or semi-human ancestors he had the immense task of harmonising his spiritual and intellectual powers with his animal instincts and vitality. It is a task in which he has failed conspicuously. The enormous development of human intelligence and the increasing mastery of his physical environment has been accompanied by a loss of touch with his body and his animality. Consequently though he has acquired wealth unimaginable to his ancestors he is unhappy. Men and women are restless and worried and the human race is torn by quarrelling and bitter feuds. Peace and harmony can be achieved in the individual personality only if the conscious intelligence submits to a principle of order, an inner wisdom, which belongs as much to the body, the instincts and the emotions as to the conscious mind. As we have seen, this principle of order has been named by Jung the archetype of the Self. He understood it to be an inherited and ingrained tendency towards order in all men and women. It is a tendency which can be blocked and thwarted but cannot be got rid of. It could be called the image of God in man. One of the ways in which this principle of order operates is as a balancing force within the personality. It compensates the one-sidedness of a person's thoughts, aims and attitudes. It can cause a pendulum swing in a person's feelings, from elation to depression and back again, or from a concentration of interest and energy on affairs outside him to a need to retire into solitude. God's providential guidance of men and women is best understood as worked through this inner principle of order. So long as we do not much diverge from its secret, guiding influence, we may be totally unaware of being guided; but if we act against this inner wisdom we are made to feel its effects, though without understanding their cause. We set to work on something which usually absorbs all our interest and we find we cannot concentrate on it. We plan some project full of hope, expecting to enjoy it, only to be seized later by an obstinate reluctance to make a beginning. We cannot be wholly one in ourselves or at peace with others unless we submit to this guidance from the centre of our being. The centre is the compass which, if we will steer where it points, will lead us to our heart's desire. Our worst misfortune is our inability or our unwillingness to read this compass and follow its directions. The inability is chiefly the consequence of our past, both our own individual past and the past of the race.

Some of the problems which dog a person all through life arise in infancy or early childhood. In responding to the requirements and expectations of parents and others a child tends to develop an outlook and to form habits which help him to cope with the immediate situation but may handicap him later on, if he does not change them. Thus a sensitive child trying to live up to the over-exacting demands of parents may acquire a habit of expecting to fail and a feeling of being no good. Another child subject to physical bullying by an elder brother or verbal bullying by father or mother may develop an attitude of timidity which will become second nature to him. There are a number of emotional habits which unless faced and overcome can greatly diminish a person. Two of these are those just referred to, the sense of inferiority and an exaggerated fearfulness. Two more are the tendency to fly into a rage when provoked, and a morbid sense of guilt. None of these emotions or emotional attitudes are through and through evil; each is an exaggeration or mis-development of something at bottom good and valuable. The sense of being no good, that one is certain to fail, which often leads a person unconsciously to engineer failure, is the exaggeration of a proper modesty, of a realistic consciousness of our limitations which normally should help achievement. Fear, though when exaggerated can completely unman a person, is an instinct necessary to our survival in an unsafe world; sensitivity to danger can alert us to take measures to avert or counter it. Rage when openly expressed can be highly destructive and, when bottled up and unexpressed, can cause acute depression; but anger has been called one of the sinews of the soul and under control it supplies strength and determination to the virtues of fortitude, courage, perseverance and patience. The morbid sense of guilt, the feeling of being bad or to blame, without having done or left undone anything which could reasonably account for it, is a damaging disability, which can cast a dark, kill-joy cloud over a person's life. But there is a healthy sense of guilt which springs from some clear and deliberate piece of wrong-doing or neglect of duty for which I know I am to blame, a sense that pricks me into a determination to undo the wrong if possible or mitigate its effects and to avoid the wrong action in the future. If a person is to become whole, to become fully human, he must face these disordered emotions and attitudes and find a way to change them.

The principle of order, the Self, presses a person to become more aware of his emotional disorder and to make decisions which will help towards their correction. It also guides him through the stages of growth from infancy to adulthood. In a previous book[2] I discussed these stages at length; here a brief summary will be in place. There are lessons to be learnt, ignorance of which will handicap a person who has failed to master them, and there is an optimum time for learning them. It is of great importance as an individual grows from childhood to adulthood that he should develop a certain ego-strength, or strength of character. The conscious person needs to gain a certain dominance and authority within the region of his own being as well as the ability to relate firmly and considerately

[2] *The River Within*, Chapters 3, 4 and 5.

to others. One of the elements in this strength is a personal ideal. The moral injunctions of parents, school teachers and others con- tribute to this ideal by helping the growing child to develop his ideas of right and wrong. But the personal ideal, though it will be more or less coloured by expanding moral perceptions, is something much larger and more specific than the aim to become a good man or woman. It will be shaped by the persons a boy or girl is acquainted with, by his favourite television personalities, and, if he is a reader, by the characters he has met in novels or the pages of history. If he grows up in a Christian home his ideal is likely to be influenced by the character and teaching of Jesus as portrayed in the gospels. It is also likely to be coloured by a sense of the dignity of unselfishness and service to others and some sense of the obli- gation to acknowledge and reverence God. Most of those who grow up in a predominantly Christian culture, even where Christian belief is not professed in the home, will be influenced by such ideals as these.

A person's ideal makes it necessary for him to reject or suppress desires, impulses and interests which clash with the ideal; the more strongly the ideal is held the firmer will be the rejection of what contradicts it. These rejected elements of the personality will tend to develop a life of their own; they will express themselves in dreams and fantasies, and they will interfere with a person's conscious intentions in the shape of temptations to arrogance, anger, idleness, lust etc. It is important that these temptations should be resisted. In the analogy I have used earlier the king must learn to govern his country and must not allow dissident elements to usurp power over it. Jung has given the name, shadow, to the rejected elements of the personality, for they are caused by the light of the consciously held ideal. In dreams the shadow often appears in the guise of a tramp or foreigner or of some disreputable relation of the dreamer whom he is unable to shake off. At the same time Jung insists on the need to confront without rejecting the shadow side, if a person is to develop his humanity fully. For notwithstanding all appearances the rejected elements are not fundamentally evil; rather they are impulses and urges which are potentially good and have taken on the character of evil only because they have been excluded from consciousness so far as that proved possible.

2

To return once more to the illustration of a king and his country it is necessary for the king first to assert his authority throughout his realm over rebel elements in it and then, his authority established, he must meet the disgruntled factions, listen to their grievances and, so far as the interests of the country allow, concede what is reasonable in their claims. The conscious personality needs the energy and vitality of the repressed forces within him. There is need of a kind of dialogue between a person and his shadow side by means of which growth through mutual influence takes place. Through this dialogue a person grows in strength, breadth and warmth, while the shadow changes from an enemy into an ally. It is important that the practice of self-examination and the use of acts of contrition and confession should take account not only of lawless impulses needing to be restrained but of the human roots from which the impulses spring. This is the right use of the plummet which sounds the depths of our being and leads to self-awareness and humility. Unfortunately penitential acts can be made in such a way as to repress into unconsciousness what should be brought into the open and so to hinder growth in humanity. I will illustrate the kind of discrimination that I believe is needed by looking at some traditional headings for self-examination, the seven capital sins.

Pride which for good reason is reckoned to be the principal sin, has been defined in a number of ways, as an exaggerated self-love, as an excessive concern for one's dignity, as a refusal to acknowledge dependence. It is a mistaken way of escape from the well-nigh universal sense of weakness which infants and children especially feel and which can be painfully rubbed in by unthinking grown-ups unaware of the harm they are doing. This sense of worthlessness leads us to create fantasies which contradict it, Cinderella dreams of recognition and glory. It also leads us to build up a self-image which contradicts the smarting sense of inferiority imposed on us by society. I may succeed in seeing myself as superior to others in birth, knowledge, skill, virtue or spirituality. Any person or happening which threatens the sense of superiority I am seeking to cultivate will be resented. One of the ways I can buttress my self-image is by denigrating others. The more I criticise others the more I appear to elevate myself above them, and the more effectively I prevent my secret misgivings from raising their heads. An attitude of contempt for others and the use of every opportunity to manipulate people and order them about helps to banish the sense of weakness and dependence on others. Vanity is a form of pride which relies on the approbation of others to maintain a superior self-image. The admiration of others helps to keep at bay my feeling of worthlessness. Pride can be seen as a kind of idolatry, the worship of a self-image and the overvaluation of objects, persons, causes, institutions, which are relied upon to make the self-image seem secure. Pride leads a person to seek security for himself apart from God. The proud person may not be an atheist intellectually but his attitude implies atheism. It is perhaps the most dangerous of the shoals on which the pilgrim may suffer shipwreck.

And yet, despite its anti-God spirit, pride is not pure evil. There is a right self-affirmation which does not indeed deny dependence either on other people or on God nor seek in any way to belittle others but is content with and in no way ashamed of being oneself. There is a right self-valuation and self-acceptance which neither blinds a person to his limitations nor leads him to deny his talents and strengths. This is part of what is called humility, which consists largely in accepting and living out one's own truth. The undiscriminating rejection of pride as out-and-out evil is apt to lead to one or other of various kinds of false humility, such as the obsequiousness of the poor and weak before the rich and the powerful, or the pose of ignorance which well-informed people sometimes adopt. A person may err as much by being too diffident and self-depreciating as by boasting and self-assertiveness. We might sum up by saying that pride is an inadequate substitute for the peace and security which flow from the acceptance and living out of our own truth.

Envy is the child of pride. The envious are less able than the proud to repress their sense of inadequacy by building up a self-image of superiority to others. The realisation that others are or seem to be more fortunate, abler, richer, happier than they is painful to the envious and makes them feel dejected. The failure or misfortune of others gives them a secret pleasure. On the other hand the success or good luck of others depresses them. Envy is sometimes unwittingly encouraged by parents and others who urge children to aim at achievement which is beyond the reach of their limited ability and talent. The competitive structure of modern society is apt to breed envy in the less able or the handicapped. Some people go through life haunted by the feeling that people, circumstances or life itself have not been fair to them. Competition is not bad in itself. Without it games would be deprived of most of their attraction. What sort of game can be had where the players do not even want to win? An element of competition enters into good conversation. One person's wit sparks off the wit of another. It is the pride that makes personal success a matter of life and death which spoils competition and renders it unhealthy. People are created unequal and are intended to be complementary. Why should the violet grieve because it is not a rose or a lily? It contributes its own unique excellence to the beauty of the garden. What is the human good of which envy is the perversion? It is the generous recognition and appreciation of the differences and excellences of others together with a determination to work towards the righting of the wrongs of the unfortunate.

Like envy, anger is an offshoot of pride. Where one person will react to another's dominance with envy, another person will react with anger. Anger, which sometimes explodes like a hand grenade or erupts like a volcano, is an emotion inherited from our animal ancestors whose ability on occasion to fight with fury was necessary to their survival. As everyone has observed it is one of the normal ways in which a baby reacts to the many frustrations of infant life. If a child learns from experience that to fly into a rage is an effective way of obtaining what he wants he loses the incentive to control his anger despite the unpopularity it incurs. He may grow up with a habit hard to break of losing his temper when frustrated. Anger when it possesses a man is apt to deprive him of judgement; it leads him to speak and act unfairly, and to inflict pain recklessly. In the heat of the moment a man is provoked into words and actions which he bitterly regrets when he has cooled down. Openly expressed anger may do less harm than anger felt but unexpressed, which creates a hostile atmosphere or spreads a miasma of gloom. All the same, despite the destructiveness of uncontrolled anger, when under control it can play a creative part in enabling a person to fulfil a demanding task. Controlled anger can give a teacher the inner force to maintain order in a difficult and unruly class, it can lend fire and steel to a speaker advocating an unpopular cause, it can infuse iron into a man's determination to fight some piece of injustice.

Lust is the idolatry of sexual pleasure and in a broader sense of all the pleasure that accompanies loving. Pleasure has been called the bloom which grows on the actions which nature intends. In its place it is matter for rejoicing. Sexual pleasure belongs primarily within the context of marriage and is nature's way of strengthening the relationship of husband and wife, important for the bringing up of a family. Owing to the disorder of original sin we all suffer a certain loneliness because we do not sufficiently enjoy the loving relationships that we cannot help wanting. Lust is the grasping at sexual pleasure to compensate oneself for this loneliness. It could also be called possessive loving. Mothers can be possessive in their love for their children, and husbands and wives in their love for their marriage partners. Possessive love is of the nature of lust. Lust treats persons whether in reality or in fantasy as means not as ends in themselves, as objects to gratify desire not as persons existing in their own right. But it needs no arguing that sex and sexuality form an essential part of humanity and must be seen as basically good. It is also clear that the immensely strong sexual drive inherited from our ancestors is difficult to control. Perhaps it is true to say that the work of humanising sex, of bringing it under the sway of loving relationships, relationships in which the good of the loved one outweighs the lover's pleasure, is one of the greatest tasks which mankind must carry out if it is to achieve its destiny, man fully humanised and at one with his Maker. Perhaps historically we have tended to alternate between periods when too much licence has been given to the exuberance of instinct and periods when society has imposed excessive restraint upon it.

Gluttony at first sight looks like a survival from our animal ancestry. Certainly the urgent drive to search for food is one of the most powerful of animal instincts. But in fact excessive eating such as is common to man is rarely if ever found among animals, except in those domesticated by man and so influenced by him. Men and women commonly overeat, at least in countries where there is an abundance of food, to fill the void caused by loneliness or boredom. This is even truer of excessive drinking. 'The gin shop is the quickest way out of Manchester.' Eating and drinking, despite excess, are clearly good and necessary. This is seen conspicuously when food and drink are shared in a meal between friends or in a family. It is not without reason that heaven has been likened to a feast.

Covetousness is the undue desire to possess. It gives to money or possessions, which are essentially only means to living, the value of ends, of objects to be clung to for their own sake. It can be powered by more than one motive. Avarice, like pride, can be an attempt to escape from the painful sense of insignificance and of dependence on the whim of others. The power which money gives and the wealth which surrounds a rich man can help a person to maintain the image of his own superiority. But like lust, the urge to possess may have as its underlying motive the desire to escape from loneliness, from the fear of being unloved or even of being unlovable. Money it is felt can buy friendship, though in fact it is singularly unsuccessful in doing this. For the rich, though they can buy the company of their fellows, become painfully aware that their so-called friends love their money and the comfort it can obtain more than themselves. Wealth, especially when sought diligently and acquired with effort, tends to separate those who have it from those who have not. It makes the poor envious and the rich defensive. Covetousness has been called idolatry, for it has a unique power of blinding men to their dependence on God and their need to love and be loved by their fellows. The splash of wealth can distract the rich from the needs of the poor and make them forget their humanity. Wealth also appears to be a source of perpetual anxiety. Our Western world has been called an acquisitive society because its economic system, for its efficient working, seems to require the constant stimulation, by means of advertising for example, of the desire to possess more and more. Nevertheless, despite all that can be said against either human avarice or the capitalist system, both possessions and money are means to the enhancement of human life. Seen as servants of human welfare they are to be valued. But recognised as powerful servants, ever liable to usurp the position of master, they need to be kept firmly in their subordinate place. We live at a time when science and technology have together enabled men to create immense wealth. It may be that the future of human life on this planet depends on the wisdom and determination really to subordinate the new-found wealth to the well-being of the race.

Sloth or accidie, to give it its ancient name, is the last of the seven capital sins. It refers to something more than mere physical self-indulgence; it is a lethargy of the spirit, a weariness of life, a boredom in which nothing seems worth while. Frank Lake[3] has shown the close resemblance between the symptoms of accidie as outlined by the old ascetic writers and those which the modern

[3] *Clinical Theology*, Darton, Longman and Todd 1966.

psychotherapist associates with depression. Doctors now recognise that depression can be a disease which requires medical treatment. But there is a normal depression which often succeeds a burst of activity in which much nervous energy has been expended, or some big disappointment or painful bereavement. It is as though a black dog lurks within some people waiting its opportunity to leap out and occupy the centre of the mental stage. The old writers recognised that underneath accidie there lived the demon of bottled-up rage. When a person who has for long restrained his anger under severe provocation of a sudden completely loses his temper he often experiences a wild lifting of his spirits. It is often the inability to express anger openly that is the prime cause of depression. If sloth is often linked with bottled-up anger, it can also be allied with pride. So long as I maintain a masterly inactivity I can cling to my picture of myself as a person of great talents. If I were to act, this picture might be shattered; therefore better do nothing. By inactivity I can keep up my sense of superiority to all the people who run around trying to make themselves important. Many evils have been tolerated because those who could have put an end to them were too lazy to act. All the same, sloth is not wholly evil, or rather, it is the corruption of an attitude potentially good. The world is not merely something to be exploited and used; it is something to be appreciated and delighted in; to those whose ears are open it can speak of the Creator who made it. It is good sometimes just to stand and stare. There is a creative leisure out of which is born the vision which makes action fruitful. Perhaps this creative, contemplative leisure is what the world above all needs today. It is the true answer to the boredom which has been called public enemy number one in the contemporary world.

3

This account of the seven capital sins makes it evident that they are one and all corruptions and faulty developments of tendencies which are potentially good. To return to our analogy, they are the interests and pressure groups within his kingdom which the king must learn to understand and manage. A policy of repression will not do, for there are creative energies within the clamant factions which are needed in the interests of the kingdom. Some restraint is equally important, for one or other of the pressure groups could easily seize undue influence. The king needs a combination of wisdom and firmness which he will find only if he seeks it from the Spirit who dwells in the secret sanctuary in the heart of the kingdom. For the Spirit is in intimate touch with all that is going on throughout the country as well as with the king's own secret thoughts. The Spirit is an inner ally who will enable the king to solve all his problems if only he can bring himself to submit to the Spirit's guidance. A large part of the difficulty which the king has in ruling his country is due to the excessive influence of the friends he has grown up with. The Spirit will lead him to choose from his kingdom ministers who will counter the old influence and enable him to identify himself more completely with all his people. The choice will be painful and the king will be tempted to ignore the Spirit's counsel.

Despite the limitations of my analogy it will have served its purpose if it has helped to suggest the complexity of the Christian pilgrimage and especially of the way of purgation. The king, as we have seen, corresponds to the conscious person, the executive agent of the total personality. The Spirit corresponds to what Jung has called the Self, the unifying force pressing a person to accept and live out his own truth, the force through which, I believe, the Holy Spirit himself guides us. It is through the pressure and the pull of this unifying force that a person most easily becomes aware of God; and it is through it that God strengthens and guides a person without infringing on his freedom to choose his own way. The turning of the king to this inner counsellor corresponds to a person's turning to God for help in the management of his life. For the God to whom the believer prays is both immanent within him and transcendent over him, is present in the soul's centre and also in the world and the people outside him.

I believe that Christian teaching has sometimes been too simple and undiscriminating in what it has said about the conflict with sin. For to tell people when facing their moral failures just to confess their fault and ask forgiveness may be to oversimplify something very complex. How am I to discriminate between a right self-affirmation, the firm expression of what I really feel and truly am, and the arrogance which asserts itself in order to bolster up self-importance? And if a right self-affirmation and a wrong arrogance intermingle in my attitude and actions, how am I to disown and reject what is wrong without at the same time rejecting the right which is mixed up with it? For in my own case, it is impossible for me to see where right self-affirmation shades into self-assertive arrogance. If I simply blame myself and ask forgiveness I may unknowingly be using my act of penitence to repress something basically good. By trying to root out the tares I may root out the good wheat with them. Again, how am I to distinguish the right anger and indignation at some piece of gross injustice to another from my tendency to get angry with everything that conflicts with my wishes? The spurt of anger is necessary to mobilise the energy I need to combat the injustice but it will very likely carry me away into speaking with excessive vehemence and inflicting pain unjustly. Righteous and unrighteous wrath are inextricably intermingled.

For this reason I believe that, as a general rule, the weight of my prayer when I turn to God to acknowledge my failure should rest neither on self-blame nor on petition for forgiveness but on my overarching need for divine help, for wisdom to see and strength to do what is right. An old but familiar prayer perfectly expresses this need; 'O God, forasmuch as without thee we are not able to please thee, mercifully grant that thy Holy Spirit may in all things direct and rule our hearts.' In this prayer I acknowledge my weakness and so open the door to receive divine strength; I acknowledge my ignorance and so open my heart to the light of divine wisdom. The king by acknowledging the bankruptcy of his own resources takes down the barriers which hinder his approach to the Spirit's inner sanctuary. I do not mean that I am in no way to blame and do not need to ask for forgiveness. But undue self-blame implies that I am wiser, stronger and more able to help myself than in fact I am. My prayer for forgiveness will not be seeking the cancellation of an unpaid debt but admission into the peace of being at one with God and the elimination of everything which estranges me from him. We grow into the peace of oneness with God as we respond to his pressure to face up to the unruly elements within and, with God's help, enable them to become allies, instead of enemies, in the journey to the City of God.

4

Those who seek to discover and live out their own truth, which is one way of describing the object of the heart's pilgrimage, must first face what Jung has called the shadow, the rejected elements of the personality; for if these are left unfaced they will inevitably hinder the journey. The discipline of self-examination and prayer, by means of which we sound the depths of heaven and earth, is intended to help this confrontation and so to enable a person to grow in breadth and depth, as bit by bit he learns to assimilate and integrate with his conscious personality all that is positive and valuable in the shadow. But not all of it is assimilable; and if our picture of the human task is to be truly painted it will require darker colours than we have so far used. For it seems that there is an evil which is more than just the personal shadow, the repressed elements in an individual's personality. There is an archetypal shadow, a more than personal evil, though in practice it may be impossible to distinguish its effects from that of a person's repressed desires and fears. This trans-personal evil may fittingly be called demonic, whether it be understood as the work of Satan and of evil spirits or of powerful impersonal forces which threaten to overwhelm man in his search for wholeness. There are elements of the personality which for one reason or another are impossible of assimilation, such as spring from some congenital weakness which predisposes a person to psychotic illness, or some hypertrophy of the fighting instinct or the sex drive. It is difficult to be sure how far the unmanageable factors in a personality are due to heredity or to environmental influences in early childhood. Usually both environment and heredity contribute to the problem. Some infants inherit such a difficult combination of tendencies that if they are to grow up as normal human beings they will need to be surrounded during their early years by a care which is exceptionally wise, loving and firm. But, whatever the causes, many people seem to be saddled with destructive qualities which they cannot help.

But over and above the imbalances of temperament which can dehumanise a person there is a social evil which can undermine the humanity of men and women. Just because we need the help and friendship of our fellows for our full development as human beings we are extremely vulnerable to the demoralising influences of a corrupt society. The evils generated by a sick society sometimes reach such a pitch that an individual can escape its infection only by a deliberate opting out. The corporate spirit of such a society appears to be far more potent for evil than can be accounted for by the sum of the bad inclinations of its members. It is hard to suppose that individual Germans were less decent living and more selfish than the men and women of other nations. Something more than the moral weakness of individuals is needed to account for the corporate madness that took possession of the German people under their leader Hitler, the madness that plunged the world into catastrophic war, led to the extermination of six million Jews and the cruel inhumanities of Auschwitz and Buchenwald. Such callous barbarism deserves to be categorised as demonic. Further, the extreme example of Nazi Germany can help us to recognise the less spectacular corporate selfishness which blinds wealthy and prosperous classes and nations to their human obligations to the poor and deprived.

There is a third kind of evil which may be termed demonic even more fittingly perhaps than the overwhelmingly destructive forces within an individual's personality or within society. There is a psychic evil, a force destructive of humanity at work within the area of the psychic. The idea of the psychic is difficult to define. But there is mounting evidence, which few informed persons will dispute, of an unconscious interflow of ideas and impressions between individuals which appears to move independently of physical contact, of space and perhaps of time. It appears that emanations of influence radiate from us and are received by us of which we may be totally unaware. The many recorded instances of telepathy are just the tiny tip of a vast to-and-fro movement; mind flows mysteriously into mind. Though (despite intensive study of psychic phenomena during the past hundred years) little is known for certain of the nature of extra-sensory perception and of the interflow of ideas between minds, few doubt their reality. Some of this interflow appears to be evil and to destroy or disturb the mental balance of individuals; it may be a factor in mental breakdown. The world of the New Testament assumes that men and women are sometimes possessed by demons, and many instances have been observed in our own times in which some alien spirit or personality appears to have taken control of a person. Much more common are instances of what has been called infestation, in which an individual is oppressed or obsessed by some alien influence. Psychologists have tried, not very convincingly, to explain these phenomena as instances of dual personality or in some other way to bring them under the laws of abnormal psychology. Perhaps one day they will succeed; but, even if they do, the question of whether the psychological disturbances were caused or partly caused by alien pyschic influences would remain open. In our present state of ignorance it would seem reasonable to say that it is as though there are psychic agencies external to ourselves which are liable to disturb our mental balance and corrupt our judgement.

The New Testament takes for granted that there is a powerful enemy of God and man. He is spoken of as Satan, the Adversary, the Accuser, the great Deceiver, the Prince of this world. St Paul affirms that, 'we are not contending against flesh and blood, but against the principalities, against the powers, against the world rulers of this present darkness, against the spiritual hosts of wickedness in the heavenly places.'[4] We meet here a background of ideas which is strange to us, and quite out of keeping with twentieth-century opinions. But those first-century Christians were writing out of their experience of a mystery of iniquity which it is folly to underestimate even if we describe it differently. The acceptance of a demonic dimension of evil helps us to mobilise and harness the fighting spirit in the task of identifying it and countering its effects. It also drives us to seek from God the more than human strength necessary to withstand a more than human adversary.

There is a tragic element in human life. There are experiences so bitter and painful that they can crush the spirit of the strongest, there are sorrows so intense as to rob life of all savour, there is a darkness of spirit that can obliterate all hope. This extreme testing of the human spirit is not as a rule experienced at the outset of the human journey and many never undergo it at all, though everyone has to endure some painful testing. But those who do undergo it staunchly find that it brings them close to God. When the king is so hard pressed as to be at his wits' end he will, perhaps in sheer desperation, be driven to find his way to the inner sanctuary and the Spirit who lives there and so gain the wisdom and strength he needs. It is the experience of his weakness, his vulnerability, that most surely sends the believer to God. An old spiritual tradition teaches that the road to the awareness of God runs through the

[4] Ephesians 6.12.

awareness of our weakness and sin. Some extraordinary words of St Mechtild of Magdeburg, who exercised a wide spiritual influence in thirteenth-century Germany, illustrate this: 'When I, the poorest of the poor, go to my prayer, I adorn myself with my unworthiness and I clothe myself with the mud which I myself am. I shoe myself with the precious time I have lost all my days and gird myself with the sufferings I have deserved. Then I throw around me the cloak of wickedness of which I am full. I put on my head a crown of the secret sins I have committed against God. After that I take in my hand a mirror of true knowledge and see myself therein as I am, so that I see nothing but alas! and alas! But I am happier in these clothes than I could be if I had every earthly gift, even though I am often sad and impatient, for I had rather be clothed with hell and crowned with devils than be without my sin.'[5] The modern reader is likely to be shocked by this extreme language. But if we look beyond the medieval colouring of the words and the exaggeration of a woman passionately in earnest we can recognise the voice of authentic experience. St Mechtild, by making herself as conscious as she could of her defects and sin, became aware of God and the peace which flows from his presence. It reminds us of the saying of the staretz Silouan, 'Keep your mind in hell and despair not.'[6]

In this chapter we have tried to describe some of the scenery of the purgative way, in which the pilgrim is especially concerned with facing and learning to overcome the inner hindrances to the heart's pilgrimage. The example of St Mechtild is a reminder that a person never grows beyond the need of seeking to gain a fuller self-knowledge and a deeper *metanoia*. But the intensity of her confrontation with her own evil was possible, indeed was safe, only because of her strong faith in God and commitment to him. In the next chapter we shall consider a further stage of the human journey in which the pilgrim is especially concerned to enlarge and deepen his faith.

---

[5] *The Revelations of Mechtild of Magdeburg*, translated by Lucy Menzies, Longman 1953. Quoted by David Cox in *Jung and St Paul*, Longman 1959. There is an account of the life of St Mechtild in *Mirrors of the Holy* by Lucy Menzies, Mowbray 1926.
[6] See *The Undistorted Image*, a biography of Staretz Silouan by Father Sofrony, Faith Press 1958.

4

The Sinner's Tower:

THE DEEPENING OF FAITH

1

The spiritual journey involves the progressive turning of the heart to God. When a person begins to take this journey seriously he finds himself compelled to face and overcome inner obstacles and resistances to this new orientation. The pilgrim has to be brought to realise that he is more vulnerable and his situation more precarious than he had supposed. George Herbert speaks of prayer as the sinner's tower because the person who is conscious of his sin and weakness will turn to God and in God find security. But the turning to God demands faith as well as a sense of need and the second stage of the spiritual journey, called the illuminative way, is characterised by the deepening and expansion of faith. Faith is a gift, it is the response to a heavenly light illuminating heart and mind; the task of the second stage of the pilgrimage is to prepare for the light of faith and to do what is possible to foster its growth. Modern man has a special difficulty during this stage because his conception of God tends to belong to a time before modern science revolutionised his ideas about the universe. It is not that science has discovered any new reasons for doubting the reality of God. It has shown the universe to be far more mysterious than was imagined by our ancestors. More than ever it cries out for some Cause great enough to account for it. The difficulty is largely one of imagination. He needs to be able to link in his imagination the Power behind the universe with the Power that guides and orders his life from within. Parable and analogy will help him more than any amount of argument. He needs to be helped to hear 'church bells beyond the stars', in Herbert's phrase; he needs to be able to see the stars and the vacant inter-stellar spaces summoning him to worship the Creator.

Let us picture the universe and human life within it as part of an immense story which God is telling. It is an extremely long story. Indeed science cannot tell us for certain whether it ever had a beginning. Some hundreds of millions of years ago the story took a turn of special concern to us with the separation of the earth, as a whirl of white-hot gas, from its parent, the sun. There followed its slow cooling during the course of millions of years, the appearance of the simplest forms of unicellular life, of the diversification of animal life through natural selection working upon genetic muta-tion, the storyteller all the time invisibly guiding the evolutionary process. The story takes a new turn with the emergence of man some million years ago from pre-human ancestors, and the gradual spread of the human race over the face of the planet. The intro-duction to the story of mankind has been a very long one. The believer sees both the introduction and all that has followed as brought about by transcendent Wisdom and Power. In the language of my parable it is part of a story which God is telling.

Let us look at the analogy in another way. All the characters in a novel depend on their author; all their thoughts, words and actions spring from their author's imagination. So the believer sees himself as all the time totally dependent on the Creator's mind and purpose; this is what being a creature means. Anthony Trollope relates in his autobiography how, entering his club one day, he overheard the conversation of two men, strangers to himself, who were discussing one of the characters of his novels, Mrs Proudie, the wife of the bishop of Barchester, an arrogant lady who ruled her husband with a rod of iron. The two men expressed intense dislike of the lady until at length Trollope interrupted the conversation with the words, 'Gentlemen, I will kill Mrs Proudie.' In vain the two apologised and begged him to do no such thing, but Trollope would not be mollified. In the next novel he wrote, *The Last Chronicle of Barset*, Mrs Proudie came to an end. It all happened quite naturally. She was extremely provoked by Mr Crawley, the curate of Hogglestock, she flew into a furious temper, she had a stroke and she died. Trollope relates that he afterwards bitterly regretted what he had done. He loved Mrs Proudie and had put a great deal of himself into her creation. So we may see God as caring for and watching over all his creatures, the great and the small, the wise and the foolish, the good and the bad, the believer and the atheist; he is the Author of them all; they are all wholly dependent on his unsleeping providence.

The analogy of the storyteller breaks down, of course. Flesh and blood human beings have a freedom to go their own way independently of their author's intentions, which the imaginary characters in a novel have not. But even here the analogy is not wholly useless. For the novelist tells us that his characters are no mere puppets in his hands. A friend once tried to persuade Dorothy Sayers, the creator of Lord Peter Wimsey, the detective, to write a novel in which Lord Peter would accompany an expedition to the Arctic. A crime would be committed on the expedition which Lord Peter would uncover. There would thus be the ingredients of an interesting detective story set against a background of life in polar regions. Dorothy Sayers refused to consider the suggestion. 'Can you imagine any circumstances whatever which could conceivably induce Peter Wimsey to join an expedition to the Arctic?' She would not force the character she had created to act contrary to the nature with which she had endowed him. So we understand the divine Storyteller as guiding men by means of their own free choices. His shaping hand acts as an immanent wisdom which leaves us free, within the limits of our nature, to discover and live out our own truth and to help others similarly to find themselves. The fact of human freedom means that we must picture our Author as partly improvising his story, adapting and adjusting it, both in the movements of history and the individual lives of men and women, to mitigate the effects of the blindnesses and the follies which disfigure the vast story. He prompts and persuades rather than forces his human creatures to make themselves by their own decisions and actions.

All pictures we can form of God's working are profoundly inadequate. But a poor picture may be better than none if it will help the believer's imagination to counter the picture of a universe without God which the secularised world imposes on us. We cannot understand the human turning towards God if we do not somehow discern him as the Author of all that is, and understand our approach to him as the slow and ignorant response to his prior invitation. The story of the human race is a mixed tale, an alternating movement of bold pioneering initiative and timid regression, of courage, generosity and self-sacrifice and of cowardice, selfishness and treachery; of violence, cruelty and murder and of loyalty, friendship and love.

Earlier I have suggested that God guides each human being through a principle of order innate in every individual. He also discloses himself by innumerable external signs to those who have eyes to see and ears to hear. The most powerful of these signs are the men and women, prophets, visionaries and saints, whose lives point arrestingly to the invisible Reality upon which they rely. All religions have grown out of such living signs through which God has disclosed something of himself. Every religion has also been coloured by the opinions and beliefs current in the culture in which it arose, a culture in which, in every case, ignorance and error are mingled with true and valuable insights. The supreme self-disclosure has been given, so the Christian believes, in Jesus Christ. To return to the analogy of the divine Storyteller, the Author of the story of the universe has done, so I believe, what no novelist could possibly do and entered the story he is telling as one of the characters in it. While continuing to be present in all men as an immanent Wisdom he is present in a unique manner in Jesus Christ. To quote from the letter to the Hebrews, 'In many and various ways God spoke of old to our fathers by the prophets; but in these last days he has spoken to us by a Son, whom he appointed the heir of all things, through whom also he created the world. He reflects the glory of God and bears the very stamp of his nature, upholding the universe by his word of power.'[1] The history of Israel and the Old Testament which records it was a preparation for this unique disclosure of our Author. The mind which has called the universe into existence and sustains it in being has disclosed himself in a man.

He lived a fully human life and assumed no privileges above other men. He was a man of his times, a first-century Palestinian Jew, he grew up in a simple Jewish home, his imagination nourished by the stories of the Old Testament, his stock of ideas derived from his parents and the local Jewish rabbi. I picture him learning as we do, not by infallible inspiration, but by experience and reflection, by trial and error. But he followed and did not resist the divine Spirit within him. It is easy looking back on what happened to suppose that it inevitably happened that way. No doubt there are inevitabilities in history, but there are also occasions when events

[1] Hebrews 1–3.

are balanced on a knife-edge and can be made to fall one way or another by the decisions of individuals and groups. I picture Jesus not as having a clear vision of the unborn future but as fully awake to the probabilities and seeking to discover the mind of the Father by recalling the words of Scripture, by reading the signs of the times and by constant prayer, as well as by listening to the voice of inner wisdom. Had he seen clearly and in detail the effect of his words and actions he would have been spared one of the sharpest human trials, uncertainty as to the outcome of our projected deeds and the possibility of making a mistake. We know what happened. The authority with which he taught and his growing influence were seen as threats to their position by the religious leaders of his people. He made no attempt to defend himself against the hostility he aroused or to escape from its consequences. He was arrested, tried and found guilty on a charge of sedition and executed like a criminal on a cross. But through the life, death and resurrection of that Man the Author of the human story has both disclosed the true meaning of life and initiated a movement of regeneration whose influence has spread down the centuries and round the world.

2

Many books have been written from the orthodox Christian stand-point both about the Incarnation, the unique union of Godhead and manhood in Jesus, and about the cross, especially about the necessity of Christ's death and what it accomplished. Here I want to do no more than outline one important consequence of his death on the cross in the light of the Incarnation, assuming the Christian belief about it to be substantially true. We have described the lives of men and women as being guided by an inner principle of order, called by Jung the Self. But if we are to co-operate with and not blindly resist this inner guiding principle, we must be made aware of it. For the social pressure of disordered society acts like a powerful counter-persuasive to the healing and humanising wisdom from within. This wisdom must be activated and its power released by some powerful sign which by kindling the imagination will be able to speak to our depths. As we have seen, all through the human story God has addressed mankind through signs and symbols which by gripping the imagination have been able to open the locked chambers of the heart. In Christ crucified a uniquely true and powerful sign has been given displaying both the measureless power of divine Love and the weakness and lostness of man which that Love reaches out to make whole. The Christian sees in Christ crucified something much more than a sign. He perceives there the wisdom and power of God. He acknowledges in that tortured human figure the self-disclosure of the world's Author, the hidden Ruler of history, as well as of the inner lives of men and women, who awakens men to their true condition and brings about a renewing revolution in their lives. He acknowledges Christ not merely as a two-thousand-years-dead hero but as a Lord and Leader who is alive and near him.

I have retold the Christian story at this point because in the illuminative stage of his journey the pilgrim is especially concerned to enlarge his understanding of the things of God. The journey is from the very outset a journey of faith; but in its early stages the traveller tends to be occupied with the hindrances to the journey and with learning to overcome them. We considered this battle for self-knowledge and self-mastery in the last chapter. The battle does not end in the illuminative way but changes its character. A person makes progress less by directly confronting his shortcomings and sinfulness than by turning to God in deepening faith and trust. There is a shift of concern away from the need to resist sin towards the need to trust God. For he is coming to realise increasingly that God is his only strength and security and, more specifically, he sees God, disclosed in Christ crucified, as the sinner's Tower. For reflecting on the figure of the Crucified as the manifestation of the power and wisdom and love of God is one of the age-old ways by which the Christian pilgrim enlarges and deepens his faith. An ancient story in the book of Numbers describes how the Israelites, wandering in the wilderness after their escape from Egypt, were attacked by a plague of serpents causing many deaths from snakebite. Moses, so the story runs, was told in answer to prayer to make a serpent of bronze and set it on a pole. This he did; and whoever looked on the bronze snake was healed.[2] This old legend was understood as a prophecy of the power of Christ crucified to make whole those who looked on him in faith.

One of the tasks of the way of illumination is to deal at a deeper

[2] Numbers 21.6–9.

and more effective level with the obstacles to the journey with which
the pilgrim had contended earlier on. We can describe this new way
partly by looking at these hindrances again and shewing how they
may be overcome by the weapon of faith. One of these hindrances
is a deep distrust, partly derived from society, partly the product of
painful experience. This distrust makes us suspicious of committing
ourselves further than we can see or calculate. The believer is
willing, perhaps prudently, to insure himself against the future by
not breaking the commandments, but progress in the pilgrimage
demands growth towards unlimited commitment. 'Whoever would
save his life will lose it; and whoever loses his life for my sake and
the gospel's will save it.'[3] As a person advances in the way of
illumination he comes to see with increasing clarity and conviction
that the way of death, of letting go of self-interest, of concern for
success or reputation or popularity, is the way to more abundant
life. What lights up this truth for him in the face of the mistrust
which haunts him is the contemplation of Christ, crucified and
risen. He is the pioneer of the new life which springs out of death.
He is the inspiration and the strength of his disciples as they try to
live by his principles. The power of the cross of Christ to work
revolutionary change in his disciples is something which, no doubt,
defies explanation. It is perhaps bound up with the birth and growth
of a new conception of the Godhead. The first disciples took for
granted the sovereign power of God throughout the universe. The
cross enabled them to see that power as the power of infinite and
immeasurable Love. It is the certainty that we are in the hands of
Love almighty that in the end destroys the mistrust which holds us
back from life. St Paul after his vision on the road to Damascus
came to see the death on the cross as the act of God: 'God was in
Christ reconciling the world to himself.'[4] The doctrine of the creed
that Christ is God from God, Light from Light, true God from true
God, is a development from that. No doubt many who have had
their lives changed through faith in Jesus Christ have had small
grasp of the theology behind the creed; they just believed that in
Jesus Christ they were dealing with God.

  Today Christian belief has become a problem to many through
the loss of its social endorsement. For most people take for real

[3] Mark 8.35.
[4] 2 Corinthians 5.19.

what is generally accepted as real by society. Philosophers may question social assumptions but the majority of people assume that what 'everyone' believes to be true *is* true. There was a time a century or century and a half ago when nearly everyone in this country accepted the general truth of Christianity. There were a few self-confessed atheists and probably more who disbelieved in God and kept quiet about it. But most people who were doubtful about God's existence accepted the ethical teaching of Christianity. Today the position is very different. Only a small minority would declare themselves atheists. But neither would most people adhere to Christian belief except in a very attenuated form, certainly not in the faith that Christ is, 'God from God, Light from Light', in the words of the creed. So the person who wishes to share the New Testament experience of God through Christ is forced by the contemporary world to face the question 'Is it true?'. We spoke of this problem in the opening chapter in which we referred to the commitment to truth as one of the invisible ropes by which God draws us to acknowledge him, and to the importance both of intellectual honesty and the need for faith to be seeking ever fuller understanding. It might be thought that the question of the truth of the gospel is one that must be decided before the Christian journey can be begun. But this is only true in part. Life is too short to delay decision until we have achieved total certainty. We may have to be content with the provisional acceptance of truths which cannot be either proved or disproved by rational argument. The illuminative way is a stage in which faith expands and deepens and this growth normally today marches with doubts and questionings about received beliefs. Yet paradoxically in spite of this questioning a deep trust in the mysterious Reality sustaining and penetrating all things tends to grow. Reason plays a crucial part in the questioning through which faith is enlarged, but it can never take the place of the leap of faith. For in the last resort a person has to decide on the beliefs he will live by on evidence which while it does not contradict reason falls short of proof. There is an element of intellectual risk in the decision to base one's life on the truth of Christ.

3

The belief that the Power behind the universe has disclosed himself in Christ crucified helps the Christian to let go of the mistrust which effectively hinders the heart's pilgrimage. Another of the obstacles to that pilgrimage is the clinging to a morbid sense of guilt. In the last chapter we distinguished between a healthy sense of guilt, which leads a person to change his ways and strengthens his commitment to God, and the unhealthy feeling of guilt which demoralises a person and prevents him from realising God's loving acceptance of him. This latter is of the nature of moral sickness which only a deep trust in God can cure. Often its roots are in a small child's over-identification with his mother's disapproval of his naughtiness which has led him to feel that he is through and through bad and to feel that he deserves to be rejected. Unfortunately those who suffer from this illness often think that it is right that they should feel guilty though they have not committed any deliberate sin; and sometimes they have been encouraged to think this through a mis-understanding of Christian teaching. Some people are hag-ridden all their lives by an unhealthy sense of guilt, the feeling deep down that they deserve to be rejected.

This attitude implies a denial of God's mercy and of the gospel which declares it. It is mentioned in this chapter because it is only as faith and trust in God grow strong that the ghost of morbid guilt is well and truly laid. As the reality of the love of God disclosed in Christ crucified, which the Christian accepts with his head, begins to take possession of his heart then his morbid obsession with sin slowly melts away. There are two mistaken attitudes common among those who are troubled by this sickness of soul. The first is that of those who have tried to escape from the painful sense of guilt by repressing it. The usual way to do this is to build up an attitude of self-righteousness by trying to be better than others and stricter in carrying out moral rules. This is the pharisaic attitude con-demned in the gospel. St Paul the ex-Pharisee insists that we cannot earn God's forgiveness by our good actions. God accepts us because he loves us with a love exposed nakedly on the cross. There is a true righteousness. But the motive behind this is not the search for God's forgiveness but gratitude for being wholly forgiven and accepted. There is however the quite different case of the man weighed down by morbid guilt, whose whole outlook is darkened by the sense of his sinfulness, although he never does anything deliberately wrong. He will invent imaginary sins and magnify minor weaknesses in order to justify his feeling of guilt. He has to look away from himself to the God 'whose nature and property is to forgive'. If God accepts and loves him as he is he must learn to tolerate himself, to be relaxed about himself despite his defects. Only then will he be able to grow to his full human stature.

In learning to trust God the person afflicted by morbid guilt feelings can be greatly helped by his fellows. His chief difficulty is to believe not that God is loving in general but that God loves and accepts him. This difficulty is felt especially by those who have had the misfortune never to have felt that they were loved in childhood. For our first experience of God's love is mediated by people who loved us, and where the experience of being loved is lacking a person is likely to feel that he is unlovable and therefore that even God cannot love him. The Christian community has an important responsibility to bring home to all its members, by its attitude and its action, that they are valued and loved. One of the methods by which this assurance of being loved and accepted has from the beginning been gained is the confession of sin. 'Confess your sins to one another, that you may be healed,'[5] writes St James. If I can acknowledge my sins to another and he accepts me in spite of what I have declared then I am greatly reassured. Of course forgiveness is sought from God and the believing Christian does not doubt in his head that God will forgive him but the heart is not so easily convinced. The child in him is glad of the reassurance that the faith, the prayers and the acceptance of his fellows give. This need of reassurance has been consecrated in the sacrament of penance, or of absolution as it is better named. This must be discussed more fully in a later chapter.

Before leaving the subject of confession something needs to be said about the increasing use of it in a secular context. Sigmund Freud, the pioneer of all the modern schools of dynamic psychology, pointed out that people fall ill because they are afraid to speak the truth. He was not thinking of conscious and deliberate lying, which seldom causes ill health; nor even primarily of the harbouring of guilty secrets. He had in mind the unconscious or semi-conscious refusal to admit to oneself the murderous, adulterous, disloyal or cowardly feelings and desires which run contrary to our self-image. It is this evasion of inner truth which can cause neurotic symptoms and sometimes complete mental breakdown. The neurosis is the protest of a person's total being against the pretence of his conscious

[5] James 5.16.

attitude. Psychoanalysis, the name of the treatment which Freud invented to cure his neurotic patients, was called the talking cure. Patients got better as bit by bit they were helped to remember and speak about fears, desires, experiences in their past life, particularly during early childhood, which they had never been able to speak of before. As they became able to acknowledge and speak about these early traumas, painful to recall and usually charged with intense emotion, which through fear or shame had been repressed, they became more relaxed, more themselves, more human.

One of the fruits of a successful analysis is a greater power of self-acceptance. The strong emotional rapport between the patient and the analyst enables the former to accept himself because his doctor who knows all his humiliating secrets accepts him. As a result he is able better than before to be himself, to live out his own truth. Is self-acceptance the same as forgiveness? I think we must say that forgiveness is something other than self-acceptance but should never be seen as something less than it. That is to say that self-acceptance ought to flow from the realisation of being forgiven and accepted by God. If, from a lack of self-knowledge for example, a person still rejects a great deal of himself despite his prayer for forgiveness, this self-rejection will inevitably diminish his oneness with God. If I continue to reject part of my God-created nature I inevitably shut out this area of my being from God's love and forgiveness. It need hardly be said that the acceptance of my murderous and adulterous feelings or impulses does not mean my indulging them or giving way to them, but rather owning them as part of me and learning to manage them responsibly, rather as good parents cope with their disorderly children. On the other hand a self-acceptance which is totally unaware of any relationship to God almost inevitably takes on a quality of smugness, a blindness to the heights and depths of human existence.

4

We have been considering how the deepening and expansion of faith characteristic of the illuminative way enables a person to find a cure for two deep-seated sicknesses of the soul, which hinder the search for God, mistrust and morbid guilt. The growing trust enables a person to overcome another obstacle to the spiritual journey, which might be called a weakness or inertia, or even a paralysis of the will. St Paul described this when he wrote, 'For I do not do the good I want, but the evil I do not want is what I do.'[6] He sees two principles at work in him, what he calls the law of his mind which sees clearly what he ought to do and the law of sin within him which prevents him from carrying out the dictates of his mind. This paralysis of the will is clearly an effect of inner division. Our estrangement from God leaves us inwardly divided, like the king in our analogy who cannot govern his country effectively because of the rivalry of differing factions within it. The king, if he sides with a conservative, law-abiding group, is faced with the rebellion of the bolder, more freedom-loving party. The civil dissension prevents the king from following any firm policy towards other states because he cannot count on the backing of a united country. This is a familiar element in Christian experience. We are pulled two ways. There is the pull of the spiritual, of the quest for God, of the new life of discipleship to Christ, and there is the strong counter-pull of old habit and ingrained manners, of old mistrust, of scepticism about the untried and unfamiliar, indeed of everything that is resistant to the spiritual journey. St Paul having stated his dilemma announces its solution: wholehearted trust in Christ. We have gone over ground which we traversed earlier in this book. Learning to trust Christ and his Spirit indwelling us is one of the first lessons of the Christian life. But it is also one of the last to be learnt thoroughly. And in the stage of growing illumination the pilgrim learns it all over again at a deeper level.

Returning to the analogy of the king and his kingdom we might say that Christ enables the king to discover and trust himself to the wise Spirit who lives in the secret sanctuary in the heart of the kingdom. When he is able to do this the quarrelling factions will come together under his leadership, for the Spirit is in intimate touch with all of them. A ruler should be the servant of his subjects and his chief concern should be the interests of the country as a whole. The king can only serve his people effectively by relying on an inner wisdom that has the necessary knowledge. Through Christ and his Spirit we are enabled to get in touch with the Self, the inbuilt principle of order which is the Creator's gift to his creatures. Grace heals and perfects nature, it does not override it. The new

[6] Romans 7.19.

freedom which grows out of trusting Christ and the power of the Spirit, of which St Paul writes, comes through the activating of possibilities inherent in us, the setting us free from the prison of attitudes and habits which prevent our true growth.

It is not to be supposed that the discovery of the centre of order within us and the learning to trust oneself to its guidance can come about instantaneously. It is a gradual process with frequent ups and downs, or rather it is a process which advances through a succession of crises faced up to and surmounted. Only step by step does the Christian disciple enter into and fully possess himself of the liberty which Christ has given him. One of the obstacles to the needed change is the mistrust which we referred to earlier, and a powerful weapon against it is imagination when under the direction of faith. Imagination in the grip of despair may lead a person to the brink of suicide. Imagination fired by faith and faith's sister, hope, can provide energy to overcome immense obstacles. When a person pictures the action he intends to carry out, the will to do so is strengthened. It is realistic imagination that effectively prepares a person for action. It is possible to picture impossibilities or near impossibilities. To cling to an impossible hope or a near impossi-bility is a symptom of despair rather than of hope. We should call a man, who, weighed down by the burden of an immense debt, comforted himself with the hope of winning £50,000 on the football pools as deceiving himself. If this were his only hope we should say he was in despair. I can let my mind dwell on a magical solution of a painful moral problem in which the problem is magically taken away by an act of God. The steps to be taken to enter fully into the liberty of the Spirit can be likened to the ascent of a lofty staircase. All the climber needs to concern himself with is the next step. If he attempts to ascend the staircase in one immense leap he will get hurt and discouraged. Of course to be on the staircase at all is the real beginning of freedom and every step taken brings an access of confidence and security.

In his growth towards full freedom the Christian pilgrim has to realise in the experience a process of death and rebirth, of crucifixion and resurrection. The king in our analogy begins by relying on a strong police force to protect his throne from potentially violent or corrupting elements in his kingdom. He must discard his police or at least reduce their numbers if he is to have any useful dialogue with disgruntled section of his people. For only when they are not under threat will they be willing to speak their minds freely. There will be tense moments when he will fear that his policy of reconciliation is a mistake, when he will wonder whether he has not allowed his authority to be fatally compromised. But if he does not panic, the threatening situation will calm down and he will gradually gain new strength, freedom and peace as he realises that the forces which he had regarded as dangerous are turning into an ally. In this confrontation with the various elements of his kingdom the king's greatest resource is the Spirit who lives in the heart of his country. So the Christian ascends step by step the staircase of freedom relying on the indwelling power of the Holy Spirit. It is an ascent made possible by a growing trust in God.

For this reason, paradoxically, the sense of weakness is a help, perhaps an indispensable help, in his journey to full freedom. Before I am prepared to trust myself completely to another person I must not only be satisfied as to his reliability, I must be in a situation of great need. I may have to be driven to the pitch of desperation before I can overcome my resistance to trusting anyone completely. As a person begins to rely more on God than on his own pride to control the dangerous impulses and emotions, he is likely to become aware of fears, antagonisms and hates previously repressed but now surging up into consciousness. Alarmed at these threats to his integrity he will be driven to trust God as never before. As he learns to rely on God increasingly he becomes aware of the principle of order at work within him spreading the sense of security. Gradually, with many alternations of calm and storm, assurance grows in him. Growth in freedom like growth in faith cannot be painless; it is 'the time of tension between dying and birth'. It is the steel of the wounded surgeon which with sharp compassion he plies to cut away the adhesions which hinder freedom. For freedom is fashioned in the crucible of temptation.

The growth in trust which is typical of the illuminative stage of the Christian pilgrimage enables a person to be more frank and friendly in his relations with his fellows. For it is a time of growing self-knowledge and the lack of this self-awareness is one of the commonest causes of difficult relations with others. The reason why I cannot get on with someone is very likely that some quality in him arouses a feeling of embarrassment or dislike. Though the antipathy is irrational I cannot get rid of it. The old rhyme expresses the feeling exactly:

I do not love you Dr Fell
But why I cannot tell;
But this I know full well
I do not love you, Dr Fell.[7]

The most likely reason for this kind of irrational dislike is that a quality in the other person touches some hidden, tender nerve. It activates perhaps the submerged memory of a humiliating incident that occurred long ago, consciously forgotten but still alive and active in some cavern of the unconscious, and so causes the old emotional wound to throb. I may know nothing of the cause of my dislike or of the psychological mechanism at work, and my ignorance makes it impossible to rid myself of it. But as bit by bit I grow in self-knowledge by learning to confront and not evade or repress painful emotions, I find that the causes of my irritation with others melt away. I find to my surprise that the tiny provocations or tiresome mannerisms which once used to irritate me now no longer affect me. As I clear the inflammable material out of the cellar the occasional smouldering match or carelessly dropped cigarette end is not likely to cause a conflagration. The ruler of a state is cautious and defensive in his attitude to a neighbouring state which he fears may be stirring up discontented elements in his own realm. With his own kingdom united behind him he is able to treat with his neighbour frankly and openly.

We have been considering some of the obstacles to the heart's pilgrimage, which can be overcome only as faith and trust expand and deepen. In particular we have tried to shew how mistrust, morbid guilt, the will's inertia and personal antagonisms are overcome as reliance on God grows. These hindrances are present from the very outset of the journey and might logically have been dealt with in the treatment of the way of purgation. But the growth in faith typical of the illuminative way has made it seem more suitable to deal with them in this chapter. This faith for the Christian is focused upon the figure of the Man, Jesus of Nazareth, in whom he believes the great Unknown, upon whom the whole universe depends, entered the human story in a new way, to initiate in mankind a process of regeneration. In his life and supremely in his

[7] *The Oxford Dictionary of Quotations* gives these well-known lines as by Thomas Brown, *Works* (1719) Vol iv.

death that Man has disclosed something of the Immeasurable which Christians are still only beginning to grasp. In our lostness that Man has become our way, in our weakness and wretchedness our shelter and security. He is the sinner's Tower. Through him we find wholeness and healing, through him we lay hold of the divine salvation, the meaning of which we shall fully grasp only when, this life over, we stand before God in the Heavenly City. This salvation, this wholeness, is not something to be received passively merely but to be actively taken hold of, it has to be worked out with hope and fear. This is what the heart's pilgrimage is about. In the next chapter we must look at a further stage of the journey.

5

Heaven in Ordinary:

FRIENDSHIP WITH GOD

1

Prayer, George Herbert suggests in the phrase which heads this chapter, is heaven brought down to earth, infusing the light of glory into the ordinary affairs of daily life. It is 'angels' age', it takes us into the time-scale of the cherubim and seraphim which is the rhythm, the ebb and flow, of eternity. If we are to single out one quality of the heavenly life, so far as imagination aided by faith can conceive it, it must be love. And as a growing faith is the especial characteristic of the illuminative way, so an expanding love for God and man, indeed for the whole creation, is the especial characteristic of the unitive way.

St Bernard begins his famous book *On the Love of God* with two pregnant sentences. The first is, 'The chief reason for loving God is God.' God is in himself supremely lovable; the reason why we don't love him is that we don't know him; if we truly knew him then our whole being would dance with delight in loving him. The second sentence is, 'The measure by which we ought to love God is to love him without measure.' St Bernard is here referring to the classical doctrine that virtue is a mean between two extremes. Courage is a mean between foolhardiness and timidity, temperance a mean between abstinence and excess. A man can be too generous if he gives money away recklessly without regard to the needs of wife and family; he can be too religious if he gives to his devotions time which ought to be spent on earning his daily bread. But it is impossible to love God too much. You cannot go too far in that direction. Loving God will never cause a person to neglect any genuine duty; rather it will impel him to fulfil it with something of its own heavenly zest.

The idea of loving God contains many surprises and contradictions. Love for God is said to be both a duty and a gift. It is a duty; to love God with heart and soul, with mind and strength, is the first commandment of the law. But love in the deepest sense cannot be commanded; either it is spontaneous or it is not love. Indeed it might be said that you truly love only when you cannot help loving, as a mother cannot help loving her child even when she is angry at his naughtiness. This spontaneous love for God is possible only if God pours it into our hearts as a gift. Loving is both the beginning and end of human life as God has designed it. It begins almost unrecognisably in desire, in a blind desire for whatever will bring happiness. Later it is disguised as the passionate quest for life; as the longing awakened by the commanding spell of goodness; as the haunting enchantment of beauty. The desire for God is mixed up with much that is contradictory to it, it is a flower surrounded by weeds which compete for space with it and try to suffocate it. It is hemmed in by harsh necessities which nothing but a miracle can overcome. But there is something miraculous from first to last in the fact that the clever talking animals, which men and women are, should be able to rise so far above their animal ancestry as to love the Author of the universe with a disinterested love. To be sure there is little disinterested love to begin with in our love for God. It is very much the need-love of little children for the comfort and reassurance which their parents' loving protection provides. Indeed we are and shall always remain so dependent on the sustaining power and love of God that this need-love must always remain as a permanent element in our love for him. Yet bit by bit a measure of altruism infiltrates into the desire for God's blessing and the trust in his goodness. Gradually our trust in God begins to take on the character of friendship; we begin to desire God's companionship for his own sake. Little by little our point of view changes. God's concerns so far as we understand them become ours; we desire the rule of God to be extended over the lives of men and of nations, not because life would be pleasanter and more peaceful if this took place but because our friendship for God draws us to want what he wants.

In our further exploration of the meaning of heavenly love let us take as our guide the first letter of John. 'We love', St John writes, 'because he first loved us.'[1] An early scribe copying the manuscript of the letter, in order presumably to make the author's meaning, as he thought, plain, slipped in the little Greek word, *auton*, him. And this altered text is what the Authorised Version translates, 'We love *him* because he first loved us.' But the Revised Standard Version, which I have quoted, rightly goes back to what St John actually wrote. It is worth calling attention to the copyist's emendation because it bears witness to an unfortunate tendency to narrow down the meaning of loving God to a perhaps intense piety. But in truth God's love for us when we realise and respond to it awakens in us a universal love which includes in its sweep not only our neighbours but the whole created universe. St John knows well that it is possible to deceive ourselves about our love for God. He finds it necessary to warn his readers against this delusion: 'If any one says, "I love God," and hates his brother, he is a liar.'[2] It is to be supposed that he is not here thinking of a deliberate hypocrite who makes a pretence of loving God but of one who really believes that he loves God, a man of piety who has an idea of God to which he is strongly attached, an idea of God which he will hotly defend if it is attacked. But the real God is not an idea; indeed no human ideas about him can do more than point to a mystery which baffles understanding. The genuineness of love for God can be tested only by its effects in daily life and in particular in the love of our fellows. Love of God if it is real must extend itself to the men and women whom God has created and loves. 'No man has ever seen God,' St John writes. 'If we love one another God abides in us and his love is perfected in us.'[3] We cannot see God; our thoughts cannot form any accurate conception of him nor our imagination picture him; such knowledge as we have of him is partial and limited. He seems to be saying that the closest we can get to God in this world is not in some ecstatic, out-of-the-body, experience, but in the love of our fellows. 'Beloved, let us love one another; for love is of God, and he who loves is born of God and knows God.'[4]

'We love because he first loved us.' Our love for God, such as it is, is a response, whether we know it or not, to God's prior love for us. God's love is more than the general good will of the supreme

[1] 1 John 4.19.
[2] 1 John 4.20.
[3] 1 John 4.12.
[4] 1 John 4.7.

Workman towards the creatures he has made. The natural human pride of an expert craftsman in the object upon which he has lavished his skill may indeed be a clue to the deep and intimate concern of the Creator for the men and women he has summoned into existence. But those who believe that the Author of all things has disclosed himself in the man Jesus of Nazareth have a more compelling motive for loving God. If we look honestly at some of the harsh facts of the world we may hesistate to believe in a loving God at all. There are natural catastrophes – earthquake, flood, famine, pestilence – which look more like the work of a malevolent demon or at least of a Power indifferent to human sorrow and suffering than of a God of love. There are crippling and incurable defects of mind and body with which some infants are born; there are perversions of the sex drive which make normal marriage impossible for many; there are cruel psychological compulsions which drive some persons into actions which their conscience condemns; there is the waste and cruelty of war and violence; there is the heartless indifference of some of the rich and powerful to the wretchedness of the poor. And if it be replied that much of the suffering in the world is due either to the selfishness and irresponsibility of men and women, which is unquestionably true, or to the malice of demonic powers, which may be true, the further question arises as to how we can believe that a world in which all these evils happen could have been brought into existence by an all-wise and all-loving God. It may be that an answer that can satisfy the reason can be found. Perhaps in the final issue it will be manifest that the good flowing from the creation far outweighs the evil. Perhaps the heroic which is only possible to beings who are free could not come about without the risk that freedom would be abused. But though reason may be satisfied, the imagination and the heart are troubled.

What persuades the Christian believer of the love of God despite all the evidence which can be piled up against the belief is his faith that in Jesus Christ God has disclosed himself, has given us a glimpse of his character and of his measureless love for the men and women he has created. The Christian conviction of the love of God concentrates on the figure of Christ crucified. In that thorn-crowned form he sees the Author of his being identifying himself totally with the human condition. He sees one held fast by frustrating and cruel necessities which seem to mock at his life's work. The brutal accompaniments to a Roman execution were designed to break a prisoner's spirit and make plain the folly of resisting Roman law and Roman rule. But in the folly of the cross the believer sees the wisdom of God. In the helplessness of that Man, his feet and hands transfixed, the believer sees the seeming weakness of Love almighty in the face of omnipotent evil. He sees one who has experienced to the full what many have tasted in part – the apparently invincible power of the forces of darkness. It is because the believer sees in that crucified Man an opening into the heart of the Creator, an opening through which the Creator addresses him and reaches out a hand to heal him, that he is able to rely totally on the trustworthiness of God. What God disclosed himself to be in that momentous death outside Jerusalem was that he is everywhere and always. Because God is Love, God is vulnerable. Because Love is divine, 'all shall be well, and all manner of things shall be well'.[5] After the cross came the resurrection. The powers of darkness cannot quench the Source of life.

'We love because he first loved us.' One of the truths that modern psychotherapy has underlined is that in order to be able to love we must have been loved. The loved child spontaneously expresses affection towards others, for affection is natural to him. The unloved child is unable to express affection, as a starving man is incapable of hard labour. He has tried and been painfully rebuffed and given up the attempt lest he be rebuffed again. What parental love normally gives to a child is the assurance that despite his weakness, incompetence and occasional naughtiness he is basically all right, he is lovable. It is this assurance that releases his natural affectionateness and enables him to love spontaneously. Most people derive from their early years a sufficient assurance of their worth to be viable as human beings. But original sin, which is the technical name for man's alienation both from God and from his own proper being, means that all of us, though in very different degrees, are to some extent deprived; we all lack something of the complete certainty of being loved which would release in us the capacity to love totally. The Creator's love which we see in Christ crucified was meant to reach us through the clear glass of parental love. But that glass has been smudged and darkened, so that instead of growing up and living our lives in the radiance and warmth of the consciously realised presence of our Author, we are afflicted with mis-

[5] Julian of Norwich, *Revelations of Divine Love*, Penguin Classics 1966.

givings and doubts about the goodness of God, about life's meaning, about our own worth. It is this state of estrangement and the multiple evils which flow from it that almighty Love labours to end; and I believe, in company with my fellow Christians, that the centre of the whole divine strategy of healing and restoration is Christ, once crucified but now alive.

2

The self-disclosure of God in Jesus Christ points to certain truths about the divine nature which have not even after nearly two thousand years fully penetrated the Christian consciousness. One of these bright truths is that because God loves us and seeks our friendship, he will not try to force our love; indeed he could not, for love must be spontaneous; he can only persuade and seek to win our love. We can understand God's action towards us as on two levels. As creatures of earth we are subject to the laws, the necessities, which limit and constrain all such creatures. Though we cannot escape from the boundaries which these laws impose, the laws are as much a safeguard as a limit upon our freedom of movement. The law of gravitation, for example, is an unavoidable condition of life on this planet and limits us; but it does not prevent our walking and without it we should be whirled off into space. There are psychological laws, as inescapable as the law of gravitation, which like physical laws both limit and enable our freedom. My conscious and deliberate decisions and actions cause repercussions deep within me which I am powerless to prevent. If I act contrary to some fundamental need of my nature, which knowingly or not I have disregarded, there follows an uprising from within, which interferes with and perhaps nullifies my action. Most people know what it is to be hampered by an inner force which like a constraining hand on the shoulder prevents them from acting as they had intended.

We can understand the laws both physical and psychological constraining us as one of the levels upon which God acts upon us. But in addition to his action on the natural level he also approaches us on a personal level, seeking to elicit from us our spontaneous and willing friendship and co-operation. He treats us as a friend to win our friendship. It is one of the paradoxes of heavenly love that as we willingly surrender our freedom by seeking to identify ourselves with God's will we find that some of the inner psychological compulsions which had limited our freedom dissolve, and we become freer, more integrated, more human, more at peace. Although this experience usually comes as a happy surprise there is nothing that should astonish us in it. For God is in no way alien to us. He is our being's true Centre and, as little by little we trust ourselves to him, all the elements of our nature fall into their proper place and work together for our good. A change of balance within the personality occurs, a new centre of control comes into operation making possible the integration of elements which under the old order had been shut out and in their excluded position had made themselves felt as a vague discontent, sadness or anxiety.

As heavenly love grows a spirit of joy and of rejoicing springs up with it. One of the attractive qualities of children is a capacity for joy, for wonder, for naive simplicity. These typically childlike qualities tend to disappear as children grow older. This is partly due to the copying of the sophisticated attitude of grown-ups and the desire to avoid the ridicule of older children at school. But this childlike spirit lives a buried life in the unconscious, occasionally coming to the surface under the influence of such looseners of inhibition as alcohol or under the enchantment of falling in love. As the love of God grows, the repressed spirit of childhood is released and infuses a certain joyous simplicity and lightheartedness into a person's attitude to life. The realisation, which bursts upon a person's consciousness like a brilliant light, that God, the object of his heart's desire, that God who dwells in the centre of his being, actually loves him and desires his friendship, fills him at times with a sense of astonishment and for a fleeting moment sometimes, compared with his friendship with God, the whole universe seems no more than dust and ashes.

How does this heavenly love for God above all things and other persons for God's sake relate to other kinds of loving? How does it affect the love of friendship, the love between the sexes, the love of parents for children and children for parents? Heavenly love is not a rival of these other kinds of loving, except sometimes for a time. Rather it is a spirit that transmutes them into something richer and stronger. All the other modes of loving can be seen as modes of responding to God's love for us. Of the two elements of loving, the delight in the loved person and the desire for his good, the second is immeasurably strengthened by heavenly love and the first is in no way diminished. I shall be led to love my friend increasingly for himself and not for his usefulness to me or my enjoyment of his company. At the same time my enjoyment of him is likely to be greater, for pleasure is normally greatest when it is not sought as an end in itself but comes as a by-product of something else. Heavenly love will lead a man to love his wife more and more for herself, as a person existing in her own right and not just for him. It will infuse into the imperious and demanding sex drive a spirit of gentleness and caring love. Heavenly love will lead a mother to put the real interests of her son and daughter above her own pleasure in having them near her or dependent on her. It will lead children to appreciate their parents not only as providers of home, security and money but as persons with their own life to live, their own interests to pursue, their own talents to exercise. But never is this divine love more plainly manifested than in the love which unites members of the Christian brotherhood. It is normal for a bond of fellowship to spring up uniting groups engaged on a common task or sharing a common loyalty. This natural bond was raised to a new height and endowed with a new strength among the first Christian disciples who met together in groups for prayer, for mutual encouragement and, no doubt, for friendship. The strong mutual love of its members was from the first a distinctive mark of the Church. 'By this all men will know that you are my disciples, if you have love for one another.'[6] St Paul can write 'There is neither Jew nor Greek, there is neither slave nor free, there is neither male nor female; for you are all one in Christ Jesus.'[7] St Paul with some idealisation sees all social divisions dwarfed into insignificance by the bond that unites those who are in Christ. For St John mutual love is the sign of God's indwelling.

This powerful bond uniting Christians did not abolish, however much it transcended, the natural rivalries and antagonisms to be found in all human groups. St Paul's letters are evidence of this. But there can be little doubt that the warm brotherly affection which people found among the first Christians was one of the factors which drew men to the infant Church and led to its rapid expansion. As we noted earlier we are able to love only if we have been loved.

[6] John 13.35.
[7] Galatians 3.28.

Only in a climate of love can our humanity expand and grow to its full height. We all long for a deeper draught of the life-giving water of love. Through Jesus, the crucified and risen Lord, and through the Church gathered around his unseen presence the river of divine love found a new channel along which to flow into the lives of men and women, quenching their thirst for love, reviving their humanity, enabling them to love with the love of heaven. To turn from the language of experience to that of theology, the first disciples found themselves filled with the Holy Spirit. Only God can heal the wounds and deprivations caused by the lack of love. The New Testament describes the new life when it was strong and vivid, close to its source in the newly risen Christ. But that life has flowed on down the centuries, waxing and waning like a river fed by the rains from above, and is still powerful today to heal and restore those who allow themselves to be renewed in it.

There must of course be the deliberate taking hold of this gift from God, the healing life from above. Man without God cannot, God without man will not. There is no magic carpet which will carry us away to the land of spices without our having to undergo the hard work, the weariness and the risks of the pilgrimage. And this taking hold of heavenly love and trying to let its inspiration direct and rule our lives belongs to the very outset of the Christian journey. I have waited until this chapter to speak of this love from above because its full flowering is typical of the unitive way. But it is present in germ, however imperceptibly, from the beginning. Sometimes, unexpectedly, it seems to be much in evidence in a person side by side with grave faults, wholly inconsistent with it, which he is struggling to overcome. The Holy Spirit moves in ways which we can neither predict nor control. Part of the means by which we take hold of heavenly life is the willingness to endure the purifying which this necessitates: the pruning and the straightening, the process of dying and being revivified, through which our desires, anxious and self-protecting, are set free from the remnants of infant narcissism. Only by passing through a refining fire can the need-love of children be infused with and transformed into the love of friendship, which delights to do for friendship's sake what the friend wants. We cannot make ourselves love. But we shall love when our eyes have been cleared to see something of what God is and our affections have been loosed from their grip on the trivial, the flattering and the evanescent, so that they can cleave to the totally

Real, the ultimate Goodness and the uncreated Beauty. We respond
to God not only by passively enduring God's purifying discipline
but by actively furthering it and co-operating with it. This co-
operation is no substitute for the cleansing which only God can
bring about. Rather is it the way in which we give a firm assent
and welcome to the Love who comes to liberate. By our deliberate
efforts to think and act unselfishly we draw the bolt and oil the
rusty hinges of the door which we ourselves must open to allow the
Christ to enter. The Spirit-lit flame of love at times burns low. The
conflict with the dragon of adult narcissism is part of what we do
to add fuel to the flame and enable it to burn more brightly.

3

The active co-operating with God's purifying and healing work can
be roughly divided into two: prayer and self-discipline, a self-discipline arising out of a fuller self-knowledge and deeper repentance.
The next two chapters will survey the field of self-discipline. Here
it will be enough to say that as a person finds himself increasingly
drawn into friendship with God he will more and more be driven
to do battle with the tendencies in himself which he now sees to be
opposed to love. Habits of self-gratification and self-indulgence
which at one time he had supposed essential to his peace of mind
now take on the aspect of chains which hamper his freedom; they
begin to look like spoilt children who for their own sake need a
touch of the rod; they appear as false friends who have deceived
him with promises they could not fulfil. He is in deadly earnest in
his warfare with what he now sees to be the enemies of love. If he
is wise he will dwell on the humorous side of his change of attitude
and mingle a certain light-heartedness and gaiety with the grimness
of the battle. Remembering that love of God and love of neighbour
cannot be disjoined he will look for opportunities of doing service
to others and he will teach his imagination to dwell on the difficulties
and burdens of his neighbours that he may find out ways of light-
ening them.

There are many kinds of self-discipline and of altruistic action
which help the love of God to grow. But I must now turn to the
other great means of fostering the growth of heavenly love: prayer.
There are three kinds of prayer, important from the very beginning

of the God-ward journey, which especially encourage its growth. First, the prayer of gratitude and of thanksgiving. The prayer of gratitude is not precisely the same as thanksgiving, it is rather a special type of it. For we can give thanks out of politeness or a sense of duty without much, if any, feeling of gratitude. The prayer of gratitude can make every occurrence of pleasure, satisfaction or joy a means of deepening our relationship with God. Relief after suspense, rest after strain, success in work or play, the return of health after illness, the love of those close to us, these experiences not only warm the heart but can through thanksgiving to God extend our awareness of his unsleeping care and love and so awaken fresh impulses of love in ourselves. Thanksgiving for the things we are genuinely glad about can lead on to thanksgiving for everything. The believer will naturally thank God for obvious blessings, but he can go on to thank God in times of trouble and affliction because he believes the love of God to be present everywhere, bringing good out of evil and victory out of defeat. Thanksgiving is a means of redeeming the past. The effects of past experience live on in us for good and for ill; they survive in the form of buried memories, repressed emotions too painful to remember and many habits and tendencies whose origin was an attempt long ago to cope with past difficulties. The more we are able through reflection to make thanksgiving for the past the real expression of gratitude, the larger will be the channel that we dig for the healing waters of God's love to flow into the desert of the heart and cause it to blossom. One of the ways of fostering the gratitude, which opens the gate for the healing river to flow in, is reflection on the gospel story. The Christian who believes that in Christ the everlasting Love has disclosed himself can find in the gospel narrative a series of powerful images which can take hold of his imagination and rouse his heart to gratitude. This is especially true of Christ's passion which drew from St Paul the poignant cry 'He loved me and gave himself for me.'[8] The words and deeds and sufferings of Christ shed light on the divine presence in the soul's centre, the centre from which a secret influence radiates throughout our being. The impact of the gospel is greatly enhanced if it is allowed to light up the mystery hidden in the heart's depths.

Another kind of prayer which strongly encourages the growth of heavenly love, akin to thanksgiving and often arising out of it, is

[8] Galatians 2.20.

praise. Praise is the natural language of love. The lover delights to sing the praises of his beloved if he can find a sympathetic ear; and by using love's typical language we can help love to grow. There is a self-forgetfulness in praise. There is the danger of a certain smugness and self-satisfaction creeping into a person's mind as he reflects on his blessings, his good fortune. The spirit of praise sweeps all self-congratulation away by turning our hearts away from our personal concerns to contemplate the loving-kindness of the Lord. Beauty can call out the spirit of praise. The beauty of created things – the shape, colour and scent of the rose, the swift and swerving flight of the swallow, the grace and poise of the squirrel, the face of a child lit up by laughter – causes the heart to leap with a delight which can be the fuel of praise. Indeed to let the quickening of the pulse, as it leaps in response to beautiful sights and sounds, lead us into the praise of the uncreated Beauty cleanses our enjoyment from the corrosion of possessiveness, the tendency to hug it to ourselves, which diminishes our power to appreciate the beautiful. Praise releases our humanity, shut in by mean and selfish tendencies, and enables it to expand; it exalts a person. Ideally the whole person, body as much as soul, should share in expressing God's praises. Music and singing can enable the heart to give voice to emotion too deep for words. Dancing too can be made the vehicle of praise. There is a lyrical kind of dancing which expresses childlike delight; there is the slow and stately ritual dance of religious ceremonial which hints at the mystery of the divine Being; there is the simple procession which expresses the joy of the Church in its pilgrimage to the city of joy. Praise is closely akin to adoration. Both are God-centred and each needs the other to be complete. Praise belongs especially to the affirmative way, adoration to the way of negation. Praise responds to the bright light of God's self-disclosure both in Jesus Christ and in the whole created universe. Adoration worships the divine transcendence, it looks towards the clouds and darkness in which the Godhead is hidden; there is a hint of terror in man's apprehension of God, whose ways are not our ways nor his thoughts our thoughts; adoration approaches God with awe and holy fear. All prayer to be genuine must contain a tincture of adoration. Without some awareness of the divine darkness praise will be shallow.

The third kind of prayer which especially fosters the growth of heavenly love is the prayer of self-surrender to God's will. This has sometimes been called the prayer of resignation. But the word resignation today carries the suggestion of a limp acquiescence in the inevitable not the positive embracing of God's purpose which it should mean. There is a difficulty, however, in the idea of God's will which must be faced. The problem arises not simply from our profound ignorance of the mind of God but from the fact that we are forced to see two different but often confused meanings in the divine will. There is first the absolute will of God who has disclosed himself as Love, who desires good and not evil, who is against the wickedness of men and demons, who grieves at human sin and wretchedness. But there is what may be called the permissive will of God, the Author of all that is. Nothing in the universe can happen without God's permission, and therefore nothing falls outside God's permissive will. To over-simplify an immensely complex subject, which we have touched on earlier in this book, God wills human freedom and therefore in a sense all the evil as well as all the good which flows from men's decisions and actions. Murder, treachery and rape, Belsen and Buchenwald, all are allowed by God and so fall within his will. But God who permits evil because he has left his creatures free is all the time labouring to bring good out of the evil so that his absolute will may triumph over the evil which he has allowed.

For evil is something potentially good that has become twisted and perverted, and what has been damaged can in principle be healed and rectified. Persons who are able to see God's love behind the tyranny of selfish men and the pressure of harsh circumstances and to endure tribulation without bitterness co-operate with God in his divine work of redeeming evil. We can perceive this truth only because it was demonstrated and lived out by Jesus Christ. We see it most clearly in the account of the agony of Jesus in the garden of Gethsemane. There Jesus prayed, 'Father, all things are possible to thee; remove this cup from me; yet not what I will but what thou wilt.'[9] In that prayer a whole theology of surrender and self-sacrifice is encapsulated. There is no pretence of being superior to the crude reality and tyranny of evil, to the shrinking of the nerves from bodily torture, to the crushing weight of apparent total failure, to the rebellion of young and vigorous life against death. The prayer also expresses Christ's human ignorance of God's will.

[9] Mark 14.36.

Perhaps there might be some other way by which the redemptive will of the Father could be brought about. But having given expression to his human shrinking and fear he goes on to declare his wholehearted surrender to the unknown will of the Father. Looking back in the light of all that has flowed from Christ's death we can see the power of self-surrender to the will of God to enable evil to be redeemed.

In the prayer of Gethsemane out of the deep of human affliction we are given a pattern for the prayer of surrender applicable to all times and seasons. First we bring to the forefront of our minds the event we dread or the object we greatly hope for, we bring our hopes and fears as honestly as we are able into the presence of God, and then we surrender them to God, leaving the issue to his unknown will, trusting him come what may. There are times when we are so weighed down by fear or depression that we can scarcely do more than go through the motions of surrender; but the more we can leave our cares and fears gladly in the hands of God the more we shall encourage the growth of heavenly love. In Charles Williams' missionary play, *The House of the Octopus*,[10] published posthumously, there comes a point of crisis when one of the characters addresses a great angelic figure, typifying the Holy Spirit, 'We can still pray that things will come right,' and the Holy Spirit answers, 'That is always the one thing past praying for. Pray that you may enjoy things going right and you will find it very simple.' This is austere teaching. Things which come right in the end may be very painful in the short run. All the same those who are strongly committed are able to rejoice even in the midst of pain and trouble because they believe that by their willing acceptance of God's will in it they are able to co-operate in the divine work of bringing good out of evil. Sometimes also heavenly love can so take possession of a person that he is glad and spontaneously rejoices to suffer something for God, his Friend. A special form of the prayer of self-surrender is intercession. Christ is recorded as praying, 'For their sake I consecrate myself.'[11] The words imply a self-offering on behalf of others which is what intercession is. But the subject is so important as to demand a chapter to itself.

[10] *Collected Plays of Charles Williams*, O.U.P. 1963.
[11] John 17.19.

4

There is another kind of prayer typical of the unitive way of which I have so far said nothing, the prayer of contemplation. As I devoted a whole chapter of *The River Within*[12] to it I do not wish to deal with it at length here. The mind can work actively and passively. We can reason and argue, we can analyse and plan: but we can also listen and look, we can be receptive, we can open ourselves to what is around us or within, we can let intuition have full rein. In contemplation the mind works passively, intuitively. We can respond to God actively by expressive prayer, by petition and confession, by praise and thanksgiving, by surrendering our wills to God's will. We can also respond passively, contemplation is a waiting on God, a looking towards him, a listening, a loving attention to him. All real prayer as we have seen is a response, it is Spirit-inspired whether this is realised to be so or not. But in contemplation there is some realisation of God's presence activating it from within, a secret urge towards God like a flame which sometimes burns so low as to be almost imperceptible and sometimes burns brightly. It is this inner flame of heavenly aspiration which enables a person to remain in the waiting, listening attitude of contemplation. This prayer of Godward aspiration is typical of the unitive way, when it may draw to itself movements of praise and gratitude, trust and self-surrender and fuse them into a non-verbal loving attention to God. This Spirit-inspired intuitive prayer usually begins during the illuminative stage of the pilgrimage when a kind of contemplation called by St Teresa, the sixteenth-century Spanish teacher of prayer, the prayer of quiet, is normal. In the prayer of quiet the Godward aspiration is not strong enough to prevent a person's being hampered by trains of thought about all manner of things, while the imagination may roam about uncontrolled. St Teresa's advice to one in this state of prayer is to ignore and not worry about these distractions and quietly attend to the secret flame burning in the heart. Some people are drawn to this contemplative mode of prayer at the very outset when they are preoccupied with the battle with inner hindrances to the pilgrimage. More must be said about this when we consider in further detail the guidance people need in prayer.

[12]Darton, Longman & Todd 1978.

Side by side with the passive, contemplative type of prayer there goes a kind of passive purifying which re-orders a person's desires, hopes and fears. There is a necessary stripping away of the hindrances to heavenly love which only the hidden working of the Holy Spirit can bring about. Perhaps the most essential part of the prayer of surrender spoken of earlier is the patient and if possible glad endurance of this cleansing action of God. This purifying discipline has been likened to the onset of night. The truth of God and the reality of religion which had seemed self-evident in the daytime disappear in the darkness of the night. A person is liable to be haunted by such questions as 'Does God exist?' or 'Is religion true?'. Beliefs which had once seemed certain and important now seem meaningless; the symbols which once spoke with power seem to have gone dead. The old spiritual guides are familiar with and reassuring about this experience of darkness. There are no grounds for alarm. The person becomes profoundly conscious of his weakness, his ignorance, his dependence, but below the level of consciousness God is at work cleansing the roots of desire. Presently he begins to feel a deep and urgent longing towards a Presence of which his head knows nothing but which his heart senses to be near. He must wait for a deeper oneness with God which will come as surely as day follows night. He is in the winter and must wait for the warmth of spring which will rouse the seeds of life sleeping under the frost and snow. He is in a waste land, parched for want of water, waiting for the rain. During the waiting, and as a result of its discipline, a person becomes firmly grounded in the genuine humility which springs from the conviction of total dependence on God. He becomes wonderfully gentle and compassionate towards other people's weaknesses and faults because his own trials make him identify in sympathy with all weakness and temptation. He becomes wise with the directness and simplicity of those who are set free from considerations of self-interest and can view people and affairs objectively. The trials by which God cleanses the heart from the obstacles to its pilgrimage are not only interior trials caused by feelings of loneliness, doubt, depression, or a sense of worthlessness but may also be caused by external circumstances – the coming to nothing of the labour of years, the hostility of enemies, the misunderstanding of friends, bereavement, accident, illness. But whatever the means, the end result of the Spirit's purifying action is to bring the traveller far along the road to wholeness and to the city where, with a multitude of others, he will rejoice to see the infinitely rich and varied wisdom of God refracted both in his fellows and, though he does not trouble to think about it, in himself. And as he travels towards the blessedness he is and knows himself to be the friend of God. But we must now turn away from this glimpse of the final stages of the pilgrimage and in the next two chapters consider some of the practicalities of the journey, and first the right use of time.

6

The Six-Days'-World Transposing in an Hour:

THE CONSECRATION OF TIME

1

George Herbert's phrase, taken as the chapter heading, seems to point both back to the creation of the world and forward to its transformation at the end of time when Christ comes again in judgement and mercy. An hour's intent prayer resembles, in a humbler key, both these moments of creative power and in a brief span shares in God's creativity. Through that hour all of time is consecrated and made a foretaste of eternal life.

Many people, however, experience time as boredom. Neville Ward has said that, 'The boredom of the young is caused by unfilled time, time they don't know how to use or are in some way prevented from using. The boredom of later years is caused by meaningless time, the question as to whether there is a meaning, the suspicion that time is one of the faces of death and futility.'[1] The Christian gospel affirms that time has been given meaning and man has been saved from boredom and purposelessness when in Jesus Christ God immersed himself in time. In T. S. Eliot's words:

> Then came, at a predetermined moment, a moment in time and
> of time,
> A moment not out of time but in time, in what we call history;
> transecting, bisecting the world of time, a moment in time
> but not like a moment of time,
> A moment of time but time was made through that moment: for
> without

[1] From 'A Bible View of Time', *New Fire*, Vol i. No. 3.

the meaning there is no time, and that moment of time gave the meaning.[2]

One way in which Christians have sought to find meaning in time and in life is through the following or imitation of Christ. This powerful idea rooted in the gospel can shed much light on the road along which we co-operate with God in the work of salvation. The imitation of Christ can be misunderstood if it is taken too literally as in the advice sometimes heard, 'Think what Jesus would do if he were in your situation and then do the same.' This advice is to me most unhelpful, for I find it impossible to imagine what Jesus would do in my situation. For Christ could not be in my situation unless he were like me in character, since my character is an important part of the situation and a large part of my problems springs from the kind of person I am. One man can cope with a situation in a manner which would be totally impossible for another. Further, what we are is largely the result of our past actions and experiences. For Christ to be in my situation he would have to have lived the kind of life I have lived. A better way of responding to the powerful summons to follow Christ is to aim in my particular circumstances, with my own limitations and my own special vocation, to live with the kind of integrity, courage and faith with which he faced very different circumstances and followed his unique vocation. I shall only be able even approximately to do this if, in a New Testament phrase, I am 'filled with the Spirit'. As water poured into a curiously shaped vessel will take the exact shape of the vessel, so the Holy Spirit conforms himself to a person's shape, to the kind of person he has become with all his weakness, blindness and ignorance and with all his faults of character. The Holy Spirit fills a person in order to enable him to realise his Christlike potential, to enable him to become fully human. We have earlier recognised a principle of order and unity in every man or woman, pressing each one to realise himself, working against the attitudes and actions inimical to wholeness. This tendency to wholeness leaves a person by his very nature open to God, despite the estrangement and alienation of original sin. As a person yields his allegiance to Christ the Holy Spirit stimulates this principle of order, reinforcing and infusing fresh

[2] From Chorus 7 of *The Rock*, *Collected Poems of T. S. Eliot*, Faber and Faber 1963.

vigour into all that tends to peace and wholeness. Grace heals and perfects nature.

As we try to follow Christ and rely on the guidance of the Spirit we have to face the task of consecrating time. A good deal of thought has been given to this work under the heading of the virtue of prudence. The meaning of the word virtue has degenerated. By derivation virtue has to do with virility and we get back to its true meaning if we think and speak of it as a strength. Certain strengths are needed for the journey to the land of wholeness and one of these strengths is prudence. The ancient meaning of prudence is far removed from that of prudential, which we associate with taking out an insurance policy or listening to the weather forecast before deciding whether to go on a picnic. St Augustine describes Christian prudence as 'love for God deciding what to do'. And Jesus constantly insists on the importance of a practical prudence about what bears on eternal life. The emphasis of his teaching is realistic rather than moralistic. 'What shall it profit a man, if he shall gain the whole world, and lose his own soul?'[3] It is supreme folly to play fast and loose with our heart's desire and only satisfying goal.

A number of mental operations combine to make the strength of prudence. The wise man considers carefully before he acts, he looks before he leaps, he counts the cost. He does not act precipitately except on the rare occasions of crisis, such as a sudden outbreak of fire, where immediate action is essential. On matters of importance he will, if possible, take advice from persons who will look at them from different points of view. He will look all round the matter and weigh up the pros and cons of the possible courses of action. Then after due consideration the prudent man will make up his mind between the various courses and will decide which will be best. A man who cannot make up his mind between rival possibilities but swings indecisively from one to another lacks an essential quality of prudence. Sometimes a bad decision is better than no decision; for a mistake can sometimes be corrected and it is possible to learn from it, whereas prolonged indecision lets matters drift from bad to worse. Of course a man may prudently decide to do nothing for the present because the time for action is not yet ripe. One of the factors making for indecision is the desire to avoid all risk. But this weighing up of possibilities and coming to a firm decision as to which of them

[3] Mark 8.36 (Authorised Version).

to pursue are but the important preliminaries to the most essential element of prudence, action. Prudence is a practical strength, it is 'the love of God deciding what we ought to do'. The prudent man is one who can and does act.

The plot of Margaret Kennedy's novel *The Feast*[4] hinges on seven characters, each of them exemplifying one of the seven deadly sins. The setting of the story is an hotel at the foot of a cliff on the coast of Devon and its climax is a landslide which overwhelms the hotel. The tale is so contrived that at the time of the disaster only the seven are in the hotel and in each case it was his own particular vice that kept him there. Mr Siddal, the man who typifies sloth in the story, perfectly illustrates the lack of the most important element of prudence. He is a man of brilliant intellect; he was called to the bar, though he never practised; he was going to write books but somehow the books were never written. He can talk well on any subject and does so at length, but he will not work and he sponges on his wife who runs the hotel. He gives sound advice to one of the women in the story who follows it with excellent results. But though he could give good advice to others he was a fool in his own case. He had known of the possibility of a landslide and had received an official warning about it, but had been too lazy to take any action. Prudence has to do with the strength to act wisely. 'Not every one who says to me "Lord, Lord," shall enter the kingdom of heaven, but he who does the will of my Father.'[5] It is not enough to have the right ideas or the right sentiments, they must be acted upon.

2

Those who choose to follow Christ on the journey to the Celestial City, the place of wholeness and freedom, must translate this purpose into daily action. How are they to decide what to do? Certain fundamentals can be taken for granted without argument. They will need to get a living, they will need to form good relations with their fellows, they will endeavour to avoid what they know to be wrong, they will try to do what they believe to be right. But with these basic principles laid down a great many different possibilities remain wide open. There are a thousand honest ways of gaining a

[4] Cassell 1950.
[5] Matthew 7.21.

living. How can a person who wants to follow the guidance of God choose between them? Perhaps by the time he seriously embarks on the Christian journey he is already committed to a career or a job. But let us first consider the case of those who have no such commitments. On what principles will they decide between the various courses which are open to them?

There are several pointers which may help towards a wise decision. One obvious indicator is inclination and aptitude. As a rule a person enjoys work that he does well; where circumstances permit talents should be developed and exercised. The fact that we tend to be greedy of the things we enjoy ought not to obscure the more fundamental truth that enjoyment is part of the God-created scheme of things. The fact, for example, that a man was both active and inclined to an open-air life might be an indication that he should go in for work on the land or in forestry. Mechanical aptitude or a talent for music or writing could point the way towards work in which the talents and aptitudes had scope. But inclination is a pointer not easy to read. Hardly any work is enjoyable all the time; and further, the early stages of learning can be a wearisome drudgery. Often too the fact and nearly always the extent of our talent can be discovered only by persevering experiment. All the same, aptitude and inclination can be indications of the right path. It would be foolish to ignore them in favour of work more rewarding financially or carrying greater prestige.

A second indication of the road a person should follow is opportunity. More often than not this factor works negatively. The lack of opportunity bars the way to many an otherwise attractive calling. There are probably many in the world today who would leap at the chance of becoming astronauts, but very few have the opportunity. To begin with, in order to have the possibility of travelling through space, a person has probably got to be an American or a Russian. Then the exacting mental and physical standards required and the long training in the necessary technical skills, together with the fact that only a few astronauts are needed, rule out this profession for the majority even of the members of the two states which can best afford to send men into space. But the presence of opportunity may also indicate vocation positively. It is easy for the son of a farmer who has grown up on a farm and knows quite a lot about agriculture already to see farming as the work for him to do. A person with a degree or diploma in chemistry or mechanical engineering or domestic science has a wide range of possibilities open to him which would be closed to those not similarly qualified. There is also a chance factor in opportunity as the word implies. A man who rarely looks at advertisements may happen to read an advertisement for a job which is just what he wants, apply for it and get it. Unexpected suggestions or requests, invitations which come right out of the blue, should be taken seriously as possible pointers to the right road. It is possible of course to look on chance happenings in a superstitious way. Sometimes people, instead of using reason and prayer to discover what was probably God's will on some matter of importance, have opened the Bible at random in the belief that some text on which their eye might chance to light would give them God's direction. There is of course a world of difference between *relying* on chance as a means of discovering God's will and seeing chance occurrencies as *possible* pointers to it.

Our times have been called an age of opportunity. There is certainly much greater opportunity than ever before for those of outstanding ability or talent to build a successful career. But this is true only of those of above average ability. The great majority have to be content with earning a living in whatever way may be available to them. It is hard for those engaged in some repetitive job in industry to see their work as a vocation. It may be true that some refuse a job that would give them some sense of creativity, such as perhaps that of a skilled worker on the land, for a higher paid but boring and repetitive job in the motor industry. But there are not enough creative jobs to go around, and many will find the idea of vocation meaningful only outside the sphere of their job, in domestic life and the care of a family, in some voluntary work in their leisure or in some hobby. These are the only spheres open to the increasing number of those unable to find employment.

If opportunity is one of the ways through which a person discovers his own particular road, another is the challenge of human need. Some seventy years ago Albert Schweitzer, a man then not yet thirty years of age, but already with an international reputation both as a theologian and a musician and interpreter of Bach, gave up two possible careers in order to train as a doctor and to found and serve a medical centre in what is now Zaire. The poverty and desperate need of Africans called him. It was the destitution and neglect of thousands of unwanted children in Victorian England that led Dr Barnardo to find his life's work in founding and organising his children's homes. The needs of mankind are different from what they appeared to be a hundred years ago but are just as great. The needs of the third world cannot today be met in the paternalistic spirit of missionaries and philanthropists of Victorian times, well though they served their own day. The under-developed countries need those who will help their people to help themselves. They need graduates who can train teachers, they need experts in agriculture and nutrition, they need those who will staff training hospitals. But the impulse to seek fulfilment in helping others does not have to look overseas to realise itself. The caring professions, the doctor, the nurse, the social worker, the probation officer, and those who find their vocation in teaching have to a greater or lesser degree the motive of service as part of what gives their life meaning. Then there is the army of ancillary workers which supports the work of the caring and teaching professions. Indeed, with the rapid extension of automation and the use of electronic methods of doing work which previously had been carried out by unskilled labour, an increasing number of the less able or qualified are likely to find a real and meaningful vocation in the serving of such institutions and the people for whom the institutions are designed.

Inclination or aptitude, the presence of opportunity and the needs of his fellows are three ways in which a person may discover the road along which he must travel in his search for wholeness. There is a fourth way in which a person discovers his vocation that, if the least common, is at the same time the most typical. It is the sense of inner compulsion, of inescapable obligation which sometimes takes possession of a person. It is the belief that he must follow a certain career, crusade against some injustice, or adopt a way of life, which he can perhaps justify on rational grounds but which he clings to with a tenacity which draws its strength from some emotional source deep within. The prophet is a good example of this inner compulsion. He is typical because a man could not be a prophet without it. A man might be an excellent farmer without any sense of vocation. But the man who has to proclaim an unpopular message, as the genuine prophet must, needs to have fire in his belly compelling him to speak. Sometimes a prophet was reluctantly driven to accept his vocation. 'Ah, Lord God!' cried Jeremiah, 'Behold, I do not know how to speak, for I am only a youth.'[6]

[6] Jeremiah 1.6

Similarly Amos declared: 'I am no prophet, nor a prophet's son; but I am a herdsman, and a dresser of sycamore trees, and the Lord took me from following the flock, and the Lord said to me, "Go, prophecy to my people Israel." '[7] Sometimes a burning sense of injustice will drive a person to campaign against some particular evil, as William Wilberforce was driven to devote his life to the abolition of the slave trade. St Paul felt this same sense of compulsion: 'Woe to me if I do not preach the gospel.'[8]

There are many more ordinary ways than that of the prophet or social reformer of responding to a compulsion to do some work or follow some way of life. Anyone who seriously decides to make the following of Christ, the walking in the Spirit, the journey to the land of wholeness, the major aim of his life may well feel impelled to commit himself in some special way, both to burn his bridges and to bear signal witness to the priority of God, the presence of Christ and the power of the Kingdom. This kind of calling has been called 'vocation' in a special sense, not in order to deny the reality of a vocation to marriage or to some secular calling, but because of its very nature it demands a sense of vocation. There is vocation to life in a community whose members live a shared life sealed by vows of poverty, celibacy and obedience, in order to attain a closer intimacy with God or perhaps to serve him by some work of value to mankind. There is also the vocation to the Christian ministry which equally demands in a person the belief that he is called by God to it. The monastic vocation and the vocation to some form of Christian ministry are two callings in which some inner urge or compulsion, or at least a strong belief in his vocation, is of greater importance than any of the other possible indicators which might point him to his own true path. But there are many less formally defined or less conspicuous ways of following a road marked out for a person by God.

3

We have looked at vocation from the point of view of one who means to follow Christ and is not already committed whether by marriage or a career or by work which cannot rightly be thrown

[7] Amos 7.14–15.
[8] I Corinthians 9.16.

up. But what of someone who is so committed? He may decide that the call to follow Christ so overrides his other commitments that he must abandon his career or make a clean break with his previous work. In that case the same considerations as those that have been outlined above as pointers to those not already committed will apply to him. If he is married he could not wisely make such a break without the fullest consultation with his wife and perhaps with his family. But let us assume (and this will be the case with the majority of people) that he decides to make no break and to continue in his previous job, what difference will his decision to follow Christ make in the way he spends his time? This, of course, is a highly personal matter on which different individuals will rightly come to different conclusions. Here are some considerations to be weighed.

One approach to the consecration of time is through the teaching of the eighteenth-century spiritual writer de Caussade. At the heart of his teaching is the idea that each successive moment is to be received as a gift from God; he speaks of the sacrament of the passing moment. A lucid description of this idea is contained in *The Screwtape Letters*, the well-known series of imaginary letters on the spiritual life, purporting to be written by one devil to another. 'The humans live in time but our Enemy destines them to eternity. He, therefore, I believe, wants them to attend chiefly to two things, to eternity itself, and to that moment of time which they call the present. For the present is the point at which time touches eternity. Of the present moment and of it only humans have an experience which our Enemy has of reality as a whole; in it alone freedom and actuality are offered them. He would therefore have them concerned either with eternity (which means being concerned with him) or with the present – either meditating on their eternal union with or separation from himself, or else obeying the present voice of conscience, bearing the present cross, receiving the present grace, giving thanks for the present pleasure.' 'Our business is to get them away from the eternal and from the present. . . . It is far better to make them live in the future. Biological necessity makes all their passions point there already, so that thought about the future inflames hope and fear. Also it is unknown to them, so that in making them think about it we make them think about unrealities. In a word, the future is of all things the *least like* eternity. It is the most completely temporal part of time – for the past is frozen and no longer flows, and the present is all lit up with eternal rays . . . To be sure, the

Enemy wants men to think of the future too – just as much as is necessary for *now* planning the acts of justice or charity which will probably be their duty tomorrow. The duty of planning the morrow's work is *today's* duty; though its material is borrowed from the future, the duty, like all duty, is in the present.'[9]

The doctrine of de Caussade, vividly described by C. S. Lewis, invites us to see each day, each hour, each minute, whether it looks threatening or reassuring, pleasant or unpleasant, as an opportunity of responding to God with all the concentration of which we are capable. But this living in the present moment, unanxiously but responsibly, will not come about by chance. It will require, at least for most people, careful forethought and planning. For to live wholly in the present, especially for those who are under the constant pressure of multifarious duties, demands two opposite qualities, concentration and relaxation. As Aldous Huxley has put it: 'In all the activities of life, from the most trival to the most important, the secret of proficiency lies in an ability to combine two seemingly incompatible states – a state of maximum activity and a state of maximum relaxation. The fact that these incompatibles can actually co-exist is due of course to the amphibian nature of the human being.'[10] By man's amphibious nature Huxley refers to the two worlds in which he lives: the external world, in which he gets a living, and has a domestic life and friends and interests of many kinds, and the inner world of the unconscious, comprising not only the world of biological instinct, but also the world of dream and fantasy, of the psychic and the spiritual. Returning to the analogy of the king and his country, what needs to be relaxed for maximum efficiency is the king, the conscious personality, what must be active is the people with their vitality and their varied talents, that is to say the emotions and energies which are not under our conscious control but whose support is essential if we are to be heart and soul in what we do. To put the matter very simply, we have to learn to rely on our unconscious depths or, if we prefer, upon God working through our unconscious. This will not be possible without some deliberate discipline of mind and body. For we need to listen to and follow the leading of the Spirit as he activates the principle pro-

[9] From Letter 15, *Screwtape Letters*, C. S. Lewis, Collins 1955.

[10] From an essay on 'The Education of an Amphibian' in *Adonis and the Alphabet*, Bodley Head/Chatto and Windus 1956.

moting order and wholeness within. There will have to be some planning, some organising of time to provide space for this. In particular opportunity must be found to be still, to read and reflect, to pray. Ideally time should be found every day for each of these spiritual acts and attitudes. But those who work a five-day week may find the week a better frame than the day for securing the space necessary for the nourishing of their inner life.

One practice which would help many who seriously wish to consecrate their time is that of setting aside a few minutes every day for the review of the events of the coming day, partly to plan, partly to pray about them. Some have much greater freedom in the planning of their day than others. The hard-working priest works more hours than most in the course of a week, but he has great freedom in determining how he will carry out his work and how he will divide his time between one task and another. Many have virtually no control of how they order their time during working hours but have a good deal of leisure which they can plan as they will. The more freedom a person has over the disposal of his time the more important will it be that he should do some preliminary thinking about it. It is useful to make some *aide-memoire* of anything that falls outside the usual pattern, anything that might easily be forgotten. I don't recommend for most people the detailed mapping out of the day for I think it is better to be flexible enough to cope with the unexpected. There are great advantages in this brief review which will in practice nearly always save more time than it takes. It will help to keep a person free of the nagging fear that something important has been overlooked and so enable him to concentrate better on each thing as it comes. Further the giving of the mind in unanxious anticipation to the tasks to be done later in the day sets unconscious energies to work which prepare a person to carry them out. It is as though the king takes counsel with his people beforehand about what is to be done so that when the time for action arrives they will be wholeheartedly behind him. A further benefit of this preview of coming events is that it helps a person to be realistic in judging what can and what cannot be done in the time available.

4

Something must now be said about certain spiritual attitudes or practices which are of prime importance. The first of these is still-ness. 'Be still, and know that I am God,'[11] wrote the Psalmist. By stillness is meant an attitude of quiet waiting, of listening to the Spirit within. Silence and quiet surroundings are a help to this inner stillness and for many people to begin with are essential, though with practice they become less necessary. In learning to be still, some place where you can be alone and free from the likelihood of interruption is important. The housewife who doesn't go out to work may be able to find this at home, though here, surrounded by reminders of work to be done, she may find it impossible to free herself from distracting thoughts which destroy inner stillness. Sometimes you may be able to find the kind of quiet you need in a church. Further, there is a large number of monasteries, convents and houses of retreat which provide the quiet environment in which a person can learn to be still. But to find a place of quiet is only half the battle. Many a person conscious of the need for stillness, and having discovered an oasis of quiet where he is secure from interruption, has found to his dismay that he cannot settle down to enjoy the peace he had looked forward to because of the intrusion upon his attention of a hundred unwanted thoughts which jostle and distract him. Things he has left undone, problems he has been evading, unwritten letters push their way into the forefront of his mind. Here are a few practical suggestions for getting still.

First try to get the body relaxed. Stillness of body helps stillness of mind. Sit in a comfortable position, relaxed but not lounging: relaxed attentiveness is the attitude to aim at. Then take three or four slow breaths, using the abdominal muscles to make sure the air fills the bottom of the lungs, and noticing the air entering and leaving the lungs. After this try to release the muscular tensions in your body, beginning at the head and moving slowly down to the feet, repeating mentally such phrases as relax, let go, be still, do nothing. Special care should be taken to relax the tensions in the face, hands and shoulders. A further help to getting relaxed and physically at peace is to focus attention on some point in the body which can symbolise the spiritual centre. The most helpful focusing

[11] Psalm 46.10.

point, I believe, is what the Japanese call the honourable middle, the abdomen. To count slowly up to twenty with the mind resting quietly on this centre assists bodily relaxation. With the body relaxed one can turn one's attention to mental causes of strain. These are principally anxieties and feelings of resentment or hostility. The rule whether for physical or mental relaxation is the same, remember in order to forget, recall in order to let go and surrender. If some urgent practical matter comes to mind which you fear you may forget, make a note of it and promise to attend to it afterwards.

So far we have dealt with the negative aspect of stillness, the getting rid of the obstacles to it. But stillness and relaxation are for the sake of stronger concentration. To help this either some visual image charged with symbolic meaning such as a crucifix, a religious picture, or a lit candle or, for some people much better, a mental picture is useful. This could be a picture of Christ imagined from some gospel story or some inanimate symbol such as a chalice, a sanctuary lamp, an altar or a tabernacle. Not all are helped by having a visual image as a focal point but almost everyone is helped by the slow repetition, ten, twenty, or any number of times of some carefully chosen sentence of prayer or mantra. The best known of these prayer sentences is the Jesus prayer: 'Lord Jesus Christ, Son of God, have mercy on me (or us).' But many sentences from the Bible are highly suitable as mantras as, for example: 'Be still, and know that I am God.'[12] 'God is our refuge and strength.'[13] 'Know ye that the Lord he is God.'[14] 'Holy, holy, holy is the Lord of Hosts.'[15] Or some simple home-made phrase such as : 'Lord light a candle in my heart.' The monotony of the repeated phrase stills active thinking and enables the mind to work passively. We do not need to think what the words mean; we know what they mean without thinking; they help us to become aware of and co-operate with the Spirit's voiceless aspiration. I believe that most people seeking stillness for prayer would find this method effective. The whole exercise need take no more than a quarter of an hour. There is nothing sacrosanct about any of the details of the method and those who use it regularly will probably want to simplify it or in some other way vary it. There are other methods of getting still in

---

[12] Ibid.
[13] Psalm 46.1.
[14] Psalm 100.3 (A.V.).
[15] Isaiah 6.3.

order to attend to God, and there are those who are able to relax in quiet attention to God without any particular method. But without stillness I think a person will not be able to enter deeply into prayer except in those rare crises in which he is stirred to his depths and out of those depths prays spontaneously to God. If once a day, or even once or twice a week, care is taken to become still in the presence of God the practice will have a powerful effect on prayer at other times.

Prayer properly understood takes in the whole of life. One practice which will make prayer effectively the inspiration of all a person's actions is called the practice of the presence of God. Brother Lawrence, the eighteenth-century Carmelite friar, in his well-known book of that title, recommends the practice to all people at all times. The best way to begin is to try to remember God at particular times, for example, on rising in the morning, before meals, on leaving or entering your home, or at some change of work or occupation during the day. The simplest method of recollecting God is by short exclamations of prayer: 'Praise God', 'Help, Lord', 'Lord, thank you', etc. The most important factor in gaining the habitual realisation of God is a deep desire for it. Where this desire is present a person who is prepared to take a little trouble can count on growing in the awareness of God. It is wise at the outset to be modest in what one attempts but resolute in carrying it out. If resolutions are made they are best undertaken for a limited period such as a week or a fortnight, after which they can be renewed for a further period if that seems good. The aim is not to keep the thought of God in the forefront of the mind. This would interfere with the proper carrying out of the day's occupations and tasks. The presence of God should be like sunshine on a bright day. One is aware of the sunshine and would notice if a cloud momentarily obscured the sun, but one is giving one's mind to other things. So ideally the presence of God should be the background of all we do, the reassuring penumbra of the day's work or leisure. We can at any time turn to him and address him and indeed will do so gladly at convenient moments. Even more important than the awareness of God is the deep certainty that he is all the time aware of us.

Those who seriously aim at the habitual realisation of God's presence will both want and need to set aside time when they give him their undivided attention so far as they are able. It does not follow that we shall realise God's presence more strongly when we are trying to give God our exclusive attention. Indeed sometimes the contrary occurs. In our set times of prayer we may be battling with distractions and darkness; we may even be experiencing the absence of God, which is in truth the experience of God in an unfamiliar and unrecognised mode; and then while we are doing some secular job or perhaps just listening to music or looking at a landscape we are flooded by the sense of God's presence. Nevertheless, despite this disconcerting paradox, it is of great importance to persevere with the set times of prayer and not give up.

Another kind of prayer which will be treated more fully later must be mentioned here, corporate prayer. The Christian journey is made in company with many others. The individual needs the support of the faith and hope of his fellow-pilgrims. Most Christians are well aware of this, but there are some who have a strong sense of personal vocation combined with a disinclination to associate with others whose commitment seems weaker or whose spiritual sensibility blunter. It is important that they should not hold aloof from their fellow-pilgrims. They have much to contribute to them which it would be selfish to keep to themselves. But further they have much to learn from men and women unlike themselves, who will help them to become aware of forgotten or neglected elements of their own humanity and so to grow in the wholeness which is part of the aim of the pilgrimage. For this reason in the planning of time space needs to be left for corporate prayer and worship, the eucharistic liturgy, possibly such liturgical services as mattins and evensong, possibly some informal services or meetings for worship and prayer or some activity ancillary to prayer, such as corporate Bible study.

One other matter concerning the consecration of time needs to be mentioned, recreation. One reason why recreation deserves some attention is the still powerful influence of what has been called the Protestant work ethic. This ethic goes much further than the Pauline common-sense injunction, 'If anyone will not work, let him not eat.'[16] In a simplified popular form it assumed that worldly prosperity was one of the surest signs that a man was acceptable to God and predestined to salvation. It followed from this that idleness was a most dangerous fault, and the minds of the young were impressed with its wrongness by such nostrums as: 'Satan finds mischief for

[16] 2 Thessalonians 3.10.

idle hands to do.' In consequence of this moral legacy from our Puritan ancestors many conscientious Christians who would certainly not subscribe to the predestinarian theology of John Calvin tend to feel guilty if they are not working, indeed often if they are not overworking. For this reason it is necessary to affirm that some recreation is essential in a well-ordered life. The stretched bow must be allowed to relax if it is not to lose its elasticity. How best to relax it is not easy to say, for people differ so widely that it is hard to frame a general rule. Most people's work involves only part of their humanity, perhaps only a small part, as for example a repetitive job in industry. It should follow that ideally recreation should enable a person to express other elements of himself. A sedentary worker would be well advised to go in for some occupation involving physical exercise, perhaps some sport. A person whose work was mainly physical should be encouraged to follow up some interest which would stimulate his mind and imagination. The intellectual benefits by some form of manual work in his spare time. The man who is alone in his work should recreate himself with his fellows. A hobby is an invaluable source of re-creation. The essential quality of a hobby which gives it its recreative power is its being an interest or occupation pursued for its own sake without any ulterior motive – of financial gain for example. Often the weariness and boredom of which people sometimes complain is caused by the lack of what the right recreation could supply. Energy bottled up and unused may wear a person out more than much energy expended. It is sometimes argued with truth that sufficient recreation makes for better work. More importantly the right kind of recreation helps the growth of our humanity, it can powerfully help us on the road to the land of wholeness.

One final observation needs to be made about the consecration of time and its due planning. It is possible to be too prudent. Safety first, however important this may be in certain circumstances, as for example at the bottom of a coal mine, is a part of common sense which belongs to lower order values and should not be allowed to usurp control over life. There is a place for taking risks, for playing the holy fool, for not counting the cost too narrowly. If we are trying to follow Christ we cannot disregard the reckless folly of the cross nor Christ's words about throwing life away and finding it again. Or, to put the matter another way, the pilgrimage of the heart must be a Spirit-guided journey. The Spirit, like the wind, blows where he wills; his inspirations are unpredictable. The man who ties himself rigidly to a plan, wise and prudent though it may be so far as it goes, may find that he has rendered himself incapable of hearing the voice of the Spirit whispering in his heart. There is a deep wisdom inaccessible to the wise and prudent but disclosed to babes.

7

Man Well Drest:

FREEDOM AND DISCIPLINE

1

The Christian's pilgrimage is Spirit-guided. Lit by the Spirit he searches for and seeks to realise his hidden potential, his own truth. When a person is able to live out his own truth he is wearing his own proper dress, his outward and visible actions correspond with his inner being. Man 'well drest' is man living to the full height of his God-created nature. Our estrangment from God means that our dress is shabby, stained and in ill repair. The journey towards God is a putting on the dress of a reborn humanity, a 'putting on of Christ' in St Paul's phrase. For our own truth will turn out to be a certain resemblance to Christ which is individual and personal to ourselves.

But this truth, which it is the Christian's task to discover and live out, is an unknown and like everything unknown contains a threat as well as an invitation. It threatens the security of a person's self-image and his desire for limited liability and only modest commitment with the hint of wild and dangerous adventure. He needs the wisdom and guidance of the Spirit who will provide the inner security without which he dare not venture into the unknown. This liberating security is the fruit of a Spirit-inspired discipline. For the Holy Spirit is both the Spirit of liberty and the Spirit of discipline. From the first days of the Church there was a certain tension between these two aspects of the newly found freedom. For the conscientious Jew who became a Christian the freedom of the Spirit meant freedom from the constraints of legalism, whereas for the typical Gentile it meant freedom from moral anarchy. For the one it meant a new liberty, for the other a healthy and liberating discipline. Without an element of discipline and restraint the liberty of the Spirit is liable to degenerate into licence. But the restraining rules of discipline are to be understood not as ends in themselves but as means to freedom. Throughout the course of Christian history there has been a tension between discipline and freedom, law and gospel, means and ends.

Christian theology sets great value on freedom because without it genuine love is impossible. There is an element of spontaneity and free choice which is fundamental to love. But, equally, a balanced theology refuses to see freedom and discipline, law and gospel as opposed to each other. There is a tension between them, but the tension is or at least can be healthy and creative. Law and discipline are intended to enlarge freedom. Indeed an element of discipline underlies all the higher, the specifically human, freedoms. What could seem more spontaneous than the rendering by a brilliant musician of a Chopin piano sonata? But the spontaneity rests on something like four solid hours of daily practice on the piano. Equally the mastery of the professional footballer has been gained only by rigorous training both to secure physical fitness and in the arts of ball control. So too the spiritual guides insist on the need of a moral and spiritual discipline for those who seriously mean to follow Christ on the road to salvation. The mind, the emotions and the will need to be schooled in order that the whole person can commit himself to the journey. Without the strength which discipline gives he would be unable to make the right choices or adhere to them under difficulty. It is possible to embrace self-discipline with a wrong motive. For example a man might deny himself in order to feel morally superior to others, or at least in order to retain a good opinion of himself. It is alleged with some plausibility that the Puritan ethic tended to make people smug and self-satisfied. But the fact that a practice can be pursued with an unworthy motive does not prove the practice itself to be bad. Those who are in earnest in the following of Christ will be concerned to undergo whatever training may be necessary for the journey. But since wrong motives can enter into the discipline which makes a person stronger and freer, it is well to keep the aim of the training in the forefront of the mind. The following of Christ, as we have seen, means to seek to live in our own situation, with our own talents and limitations, with the wholeheartedness and love towards God and our fellows with which Christ lived his life in his circumstances and with his unique vocation. To do this even approximately means the effort to gain self-mastery and the freedom which this makes possible.

This self-mastery is something which can easily be misunderstood. It becomes possible only as a result of self-awareness, as bit by bit the powerful energies within a person become known to him. There is no question of mastering these energies in the sense of dominating them. It is a matter of learning how to manage them, how to trust them and lead them and not be carried away by them. Much of the discipline of the journey consists in learning how to guide these inner forces. To return to our familiar illustration the king must first get to know and understand the people under his rule, both the law-abiding and the law-breaking elements, to realise their needs and their grievances. He must be able to communicate his own aims and hopes to his people, if he is to enlist their whole-hearted support in his pilgrimage. For this he will have to make his policy known in a vivid and attractive manner. He will need the equivalent of a civil service in order to govern efficiently, and perhaps a police force in order to bring the recalcitrant elements into line with his policy or at least to prevent their wrecking it. Or, to abandon analogy, he will have to acquire certain strengths or firm habits. One of the strengths he will need, prudence, was discussed in the last chapter. Prudence, however, is the ruling member of a quartet called the cardinal virtues which from time immemorial have been regarded as an essential part of the goodness proper to man. Without these strengths love, however well-intentioned, will be ineffective and likely to degenerate into sentimentality or idle talk. We could not better reflect on the discipline necessary for the following of Christ than by considering these hinge virtues, which can best be understood as particular good habits. These habits provide the administrative infra-structure which enables the king to rule effectively.

Habit plays an indispensable part in human life. It is common to think of habit negatively, of the bad habits which are difficult to break such as undue smoking or drinking. But every complicated action from walking, speaking or reading, to painting a picture or piloting an aeroplane, is possible only through the acquisition of habits which enable us to perform multiple operations without thinking about them so that our minds are free to concentrate on the object of the operations. A good man is one who habitually acts

well. Many a man who could not be called generous will occasionally do a generous action. A generous man is one who habitually
acts generously. In a similar way a moderate tennis player will
occasionally bring off a brilliant shot. The good player is one who
can be relied upon to play a good game. In acquiring a difficult
skill nothing is more important than a strong desire to gain it
together with the assurance that it is within his power. Imagination
is a potent factor in learning to do anything well. For picturing the
action you intend sets in motion the nervous forces which will be
needed for its carrying out. The picturing is part of the communi-
cations network which enables the ruler to enlist his people, or the
appropriate groups of his people, in the effective execution of his
policy. Thus a man recognising a streak of meanness in his character
and wanting to become more generous should picture the generous
actions of others, recall them or read about them, and from that go
on to picture himself acting generously in specific and not improb-
able situations. To do this would be bound to release in him
generous impulses which his habit of meanness had held in check.
The will to act generously will be greatly strengthened if it is fed
with this fuel.

The moral strengths known as the cardinal virtues cover fairly
completely the field of moral action. In the last chapter we considered prudence, the first of the four. The Christian desiring to
follow Christ will aim at habitually ordering his time with a view
to fulfilling his vocation. But prudence needs the support of other
habitual attitudes in order in practice to act wisely. Freud has
underlined, what many understood before the advent of psychoanalysis, that people can act from motives of which they are wholly
unaware. A man in other respects wise can be blinded by prejudice
when his own interests or those of his class or country are at stake.
Man has been called a rational animal, but his actions are by no
means totally determined by reason. If a man's intelligence is to
guide his actions it will have to be supported by strengths which
will bring order into his emotions and the irrational elements within
him.

2

The first of these coadjutors to prudence has been called justice,
the moral strength which recognises obligations to others and is

determined to give to every man his due. Man is a social animal. We depend on others from birth to death. Our humanity develops, we become individual persons by responding to others. We are educated through the influence of a multitude of minds and personalities. To some of these, our parents, relatives, teachers and acquaintances we respond directly, to most of them we respond indirectly through the medium of literature and the arts, through television, radio and the press. Our livelihood in the modern world depends on a world-wide co-operative enterprise. This interdependence of men and women the world over means that the good of each is the concern of all and the good of all the concern of each. What we have received from others constitutes a debt to promote the general good of mankind, of our family first, our neighbourhood, our country and the whole world. Unfortunately the individual's fear for himself and his own personal interests tend to make him selfish, neglect the common good or put his private interests before it. This deep-seated prejudice in our own favour needs to be corrected by the moral strength of justice. The unjust man, the man who receives but does not give, who does not attempt to pull his weight in the society to which he belongs, is revolting against the human condition and, though he may not know it, is maiming his humanity. The just person on the contrary loves justice. He accepts to the full that he is under obligation to his fellows and discharges his debt willingly. He hates injustice and if he should discover that inadvertently he has acted unfairly to anyone he is much upset and will do all he can to remedy the wrong.

Christian conduct has been thought of too exclusively in terms of loving one's neighbour, not enough in fulfilling one's human obligations to him. There is of course no contradiction between love and justice. Indeed justice might be understood as part of the executive arm of love. Self-forgetful love will go much further than the dictates of justice demand. But human selfishness leads to a great deal of self-deceit. It is all too possible for a person to think that he loves his neighbour because he has kindly feelings towards him while feeling in no way concerned about his material wellbeing. There are some sharp words on this subject in the letter of James. 'If a brother or sister is ill-clad and in lack of daily food, and one of you says to them, "Go in peace, be warmed and filled," without giving them the things needed for the body, what does it profit?'[1] Genuine love will express itself in practical action where this is appropriate and principles of justice are often the best counsellors for love to consult as to what should be done. Justice is one of the modes of loving.

We see the harmony of love and justice in the golden rule: 'Do as you would be done by.' Strictly speaking this must be seen as a rule of justice. It would be extremely unjust to expect others to help me if I were not prepared to help them equally. The man who obtains his neighbour's help in bringing a neglected garden into order and is unwilling to give his neighbour similar help when asked is guilty of injustice rather than of being unloving, though the latter is also true. The golden rule in the positive form in which Christ stated it is in fact a most demanding one. It demands the use of imagination and thought as well as of sympathy and good will. For to obey its directions means that I must put myself into the shoes of other people, that I must picture to myself how I should feel in their position and use the same standards in assessing their actions as I do with my own. I habitually excuse my own failures in the knowledge of my good intentions and of difficulties known to myself but not to others. The golden rule should mean that I habitually assume good intentions and difficulties unknown to myself when others fall short. Too easily I find myself condemning others on the evidence of their actions or failures to act without considering their possible reasons for failure. To apply a different standard to others from what I apply to myself is a failure in justice.

One fundamental debt owed by men and women to one another is to recognise the dignity of each as a person existing in his own right, created by God to discover and live out his own truth and to attain to wholeness in the city of God. The recognition of the unique worth of another is important partly because it is through our recognition by others that we begin to discover ourselves. To put it very simply we tend to respond to the way we are treated, to live up to others' expectations of us. To treat a person as irresponsible is to encourage him to behave irresponsibly. To treat him as someone to be relied upon will call out whatever capacity he has to prove himself dependable. To treat people as human beings, as persons, helps them to realise more of their humanity. In the large-scale

[1] James 2.15–16.

organisations of industry or of civil service administration it becomes almost inevitable that people should be treated to some extent as interchangeable units, as impersonal cogs in a vast and intricate machine. However necessary this may seem in the interests of efficient organisation it involves a violation of human dignity and is often felt as subtly, or not so subtly, degrading. A great deal of industrial unrest, though often ostensibly about wages, arises from an atmosphere of dissatisfaction and grumbling at the way workers feel treated by the organisation for which they work. It may be that the unrest caused by the impersonality of large-scale organisations more than outweighs any gain from the cutting of costs. It could often be that small is not only beautiful but is sometimes more efficient because it can pay more respect to the humanity of workers. We are much concerned today about the widespread disruption caused by industrial action, and those who suffer severely as a result of it are inclined to condemn strikes as simply wrong. But it is clear that the right of a person to withhold his labour for good reason is part of his dignity as a free person. We must add that to strike irresponsibly and without regard to the suffering it may inflict on others is a betrayal of human dignity.

We owe a debt in justice to acknowledge the worth of our fellows. One of the ways in which this debt is discharged is by listening to them with attention and sympathy. Industry recognises the importance of this by appointing personnel officers whose principal task is to listen to the grumbles and grievances of workers. To listen with attention can be an exacting duty for it makes demands on time and sympathy. It is possible for me to appear to listen when, though the words spoken register in my consciousness, my real interest is far away; I may be indulging in a private dream of my own or I may be just looking for an opportunity to break in and express my own ideas. No doubt there is a give and take proper to conversation, but the failure to listen to my fellow when he wants to speak is a failure of justice, it is a withholding of what is due to him. Sometimes attempted suicide is really a *cri de coeur* from someone who feels friendless and badly needs the reassurance of having his troubles listened to. The Samaritans organisation has brought help to many thousands and turned back many from the brink of suicide through its teams of men and women trained in the art of listening.

To acknowledge the dignity of my fellow as a person is one of the debts which I owe as one human being to another. Arising out of this recognition of the human reality and worth of individuals there is the further debt of loyalty to the various groups to which a person belongs. The quality and degree of this loyalty will vary according to the nature of the group. A man belongs to a family, to a group of friends, to his associates at work including his employer, to his neighbourhood, to his country. Each of these groups confers some benefits on him and he is under obligation to consider the common interest of each of them and where necessary to sacrifice his own private wishes for the sake of the general good. This concern for the common good of whatever group a person belongs to is a powerful humanising force and acts as a corrective of the selfishness which stunts human growth. Unless a person has a strong attachment to the common good his judgement is likely to be spoilt by personal prejudice or ambition or the desire for peace at any price. Among the most painful decisions anyone can have to make are those which involve a clash of loyalties. Must a cabinet minister resign who though in general agreement with cabinet policy strongly disagrees with one important detail of it? Should a man give up his job and face unemployment with consequent hardship to his wife and family if his firm expects him to do what he believes to be dishonest? Only one who loves justice and is deeply committed to fulfilling what he owes to God and his fellows can be relied on to decide rightly when loyalties clash.

3

If prudence enables us to order our time wisely, and justice to be fair in our relationships with others, the strength known as temperance or moderation enables us to act rightly in the sphere of enjoyment. Temperance in the matter of drinking has often been wrongly understood to imply total abstinence. But the word properly means moderation, avoiding excess. Pleasure is God-created and therefore in itself innocent; it is the reward that accompanies the activities which nature and the Author of nature intends. For the believer it is an occasion of gratitude. It need not be shunned but rather made the material of praise. All the same because of our estrangement from true wholeness and the deep content which would flow from it we tend to be greedy of pleasure and to go to excess in the things we enjoy. We are trying to compensate ourselves for the missing peace we crave and so, contrary to our intention, add to the inner dissatisfaction we are trying to escape. We search for a way out of boredom and look for it in the activities which we enjoy, whether in eating or drinking, in reading or watching television, in sport or society. All these are good in themselves but bad for us if we pursue them to excess. Happiness directly sought eludes us; it comes, if it comes at all, in the course of some action done without special thought of enjoyment or in the commerce of friendship sought for its own sake. Enjoyment sought too directly or too eagerly is apt to leave us with the sense of wasted time, of energy used up to no purpose, or even, in Shakespeare's phrase, 'the expense of spirit in a waste of shame'.

The habit of moderation is like the brakes on car or bicycle. Good brakes not only make safe driving possible but they enable a person to drive much faster than he would dare to do if his brakes were unreliable. The strength to be moderate enables a person to live more freely, more intensely, with greater zest than he could if he were continually liable to be carried away into excess. In fact, as the Epicurean philosophers well understood, moderation makes for greater enjoyment. Pleasure pursued without restraint is subject to the law of diminishing returns and becomes less and less pleasurable. In considering the consecration of time we saw the importance of so ordering things as to enable a person to be wholly concentrated on the occupation of the moment, undistracted by past or future. Without moderation this kind of concentration is completely impossible.

The strength to be moderate confers freedom, security and a sense of peace, but this freedom will not usually be won without a struggle. The good working brakes which will enable a person to pull himself up immediately cannot be bought for money. To gain them means battle with inborn tendencies, with greedy and grasping habits, early acquired and hard to break. It is true, of course, that some people from temperament and early training find moderation congenial to them and can gain it without great difficulty. But the majority have to fight habits of self-indulgence which have grown strong and turbulent, which resist efforts to subdue them and cannot be overcome without determined and persistent effort. It is necessary to act against tendencies innocent in themselves which have grown swollen and unhealthy through lack of control. If I have been extravagant in the time I have spent on my pleasures I may have to cut them out altogether for a season if I am to learn to order my time better. Total abstinence for a time from some innocent enjoyment may be the only way of learning restraint when I have been indulging it to excess. To straighten a stick bent one way you may have to bend it the opposite way. William James, the American psychologist, used to give this advice: 'Do every day something you don't like doing for no other reason than that you don't like doing it.' He likened this exhilarating practice to the regular payment of insurance premiums. The small regular payments which you can afford without difficulty give you the sense of security resulting from the knowledge that, in the unfortunate event of fire, you are covered. In a similar way the regular acts of self-denial build up reserves of strength with which to meet the great crises when they come. The ability to say 'no' to inclination is part and parcel of the power to say 'yes' to opportunity when it knocks.

Those who believe themselves committed to the Christian pilgrimage and deny themselves nothing of the things they enjoy are deceiving themselves; they are playing at discipleship. I am not suggesting that we should emulate the harsh self-punishment of the athlete in search of an Olympic gold medal. Nor do I think that except for some special reason we should 'scorn delights and live laborious days' as many a person does in building a successful career. For in the field of discipline and restraint motive is all-important. A miser may deny himself all but the necessities of life in order to become rich. An ambitious man may sacrifice everything that stands in the way of power and success. Self-discipline is a means to an end and the forgetting of this has brought the whole idea of spiritual training into disrepute. There are not only deliberately chosen goals which provide the motive for self-denial; there are also unconscious fears and desires. A man may feel impelled to self-denial by the unacknowledged fear of his own dynamism, ambition or sex-drive. He may be urged to self-punishment by a morbid sense of guilt. It is possible to go to excess in restraining our own over-attachment to particular pleasures; it is even possible to find a perverted pleasure in self-inflicted pain. All these mistakes should make us scrutinise carefully the motives which underlie our efforts to gain the strength which flows from moderation. Nevertheless *abusus non tollit usum*. It is not necessary, because self-restraint can be exercised from a wrong motive, to abandon the elementary dictate of common sense that moderation is part of human nature as it is meant to be and that self-restraint can foster the growth of freedom and humanity. Strength, though capable of misuse, is valuable. Many enterprises which could have succeeded have failed because of the lack of the disciplined determination to see them through. Again and again, the words spoken by Christ to his disciples in Gethsemane exactly fit well-intentioned followers of his, 'The Spirit indeed is willing but the flesh is weak.'[2]

4

If moderation is the strength which enables a person to behave rightly in the sphere of the enjoyable, the strength called fortitude enables him to confront difficulty and danger without flinching. There is a fighting spirit shared with our animal ancestors which in its human form is proper to man. Without it we cannot live a fully human life. There are difficulties to be overcome, injustices to be fought, the selfish plans of selfish men to be resisted. There is need of the controlled fire which will mobilise all a person's fighting energies to confront either the sudden energy or the daily grind. The idea of the Christian disciple as Christ's soldier goes back to the very first days of the Christian movement. Bunyan has given a stirring image of Christian fortitude in *Pilgrim's Progress*. Christian on his journey from the City of Destruction to the Celestial City comes early on to Interpreter's House where he is shown many truths in the form of pictures, some of them moving pictures. Of most of these Christian has to ask Interpreter to give the explanation. But then he is shown a wonderful palace, inside which many people can be seen clothed in gold and rejoicing to the accompaniment of music and singing. In the foreground there is a crowd of men and women looking eagerly towards the palace, moving towards it and then drawing back in fear; for the gate of the palace was kept by armed men with drawn swords, barring the way against any who would enter in. There was a writer seated at a table equipped with pen and ink to take down the names of any who would seek entrance to the palace. As Christian watched the people hesitating he observed one man of exceedingly stout countenance

[2] Mark 14.38

approach the writer and say, 'Put my name down, sir.' With that he put on helmet, seized a sword and made a sudden fierce rush on the armed men, who resisted him with might and main. There was a furious battle in which many hard blows were given and received, but he fought his way through and was received into the palace with fanfare of trumpets and great joy. Christian was much moved and turned to Interpreter saying, 'I think I know what that means.'

Fortitude has been called the bodyguard of the other virtues, because without it they are all liable to fail under pressure. Without its strength I shall often act unwisely when the right course is arduous, dangerous or likely to arouse the antagonism or dislike of others. Without it I am liable to evade unpleasant truths or fail to notice facts if they should indicate a disagreeable course of action or, at least, not give them due weight. Without the fighting fire which fortitude kindles and controls I shall lack the determination to resist injustice, to stand up to those who are subordinating the general good to their personal ambition or to state unpopular truth. Without fortitude I shall wilt and give up in the battle with habits of self-indulgence and shall fail to persevere in the heart's pilgrimage in the face of disappointment, loneliness and a sense of failure. Courage is a strength which all men whether professing religious belief or not admire, for it is something proper to man and is universally recognised to be such.

In a culture, such as the feudal, which gave an honoured place to the fighting man, fortitude was a much esteemed virtue. Today the frightening destructiveness of modern weapons which two world wars have impressed upon our minds has robbed war of most of the romance it ever had. Partly because of this Christian ethical teaching has tended to stress such virtues as love, kindness, compassion and patience. There has been too little encouragement of the fighting qualities of courage and endurance. As a result there are many Christians of exemplary piety who strike the observer as dull, rather discouraged and distinctly uninspiring, quite unlike what he feels a Christian ought to be. There is an anaemic quality about much contemporary Christianity due to the lack of the fighting vigour of the soldier. I have no wish to pass judgement on individual Christians. Each person has his own burden of sorrow and frustration to bear of which others as a rule know nothing. But I think that part of the reason for the ineffective witness of many Christians is that not enough attention has been given in Christian instruction and preaching to the place of fortitude in the Christian life. The way this may best be done perhaps is by exposing the folly of superficial optimism, drawing attention to the evils which are threatening our lives and values and pointing out practical ways of combating the dangers. Vague exhortation is useless, and to inveigh against evils without any suggestion as to how they can be combatted is merely to spread discouragement.

Fortitude is the ally of the other cardinal virtues, not only because it lends them its fighting determination when they are under threat but because it is closely associated with faith. 'Fear not, only believe,' said Jesus to his disciples. 'Why are you so fearful, O you of little faith?'[3] For this reason prayer, the ever-available expression of faith, is the powerful ally and support of fortitude. It was through prayer in Gethsemane that Jesus sought and found the strength to face and remain firm in the agonising trial which confronted him. Faith steeled by fortitude is the only weapon strong enough to enable men and women to withstand the cruel necessities which occasionally imprison people in our contemporary world. Heredity and upbringing can together saddle a person with a psychological burden which is bound to crush him unless he is upheld by heroic faith. The prison camp, the solitary cell, the torture chamber, the brain-washer's office, can break the spirit of anyone not endowed with superhuman faith and fortitude working in collaboration. Only a comparative few are stretched on the inhuman rack of trials such as these; but most people at some time in their life have to endure spells of affliction which demand great courage and faith, if they are to get through them without dishonouring their manhood. The anguish caused by the breakdown of marriage or of close friendship, the humiliation of abject failure, prolonged and distressing illness, severe depression, acute loneliness: one or other of these trials is likely to befall most people; only fortitude and faith will enable us to endure them in a manner worthy of our humanity.

We have been considering four of the strengths necessary for living a fully human life. They are all necessary; but they are not sufficient unless they are permeated by a quality which flows from a certain union of will with God and a relationship of dependence on him. In the gaining and the development of these strengths therefore constant and confident prayer is needed; constant because

[3] Mark 4.40.

our relationship with God cannot be made secure by a once-for-all act but has to be continually reaffirmed, confident because we are all the time under attack from the spirit of mistrust. In the picture language of our analogy there must all the time be a turning to and relying on the wisdom and the all-penetrating influence of the Spirit who lives in the heart of the kingdom. His task is first of all to gather from among his subjects those who will support him in his purpose to govern wisely and justly and to act with moderation and courage. A good king will associate with wise counsellors, upright magistrates, able heads of the civil service, of the police and armed forces, all drawn from the people.

The king in this analogy corresponds to the conscious personality which grows in strength by accepting more and more of its being into the circle of its awareness. Growth in the cardinal virtues corresponds closely with the development of ego-strength, which is one of the first tasks to be undertaken in the journey to wholeness. But there is a definite limit to the amount of ourselves which we can bring under conscious control, and when the person has become strong enough another task confronts him. This is the hazardous duty of opening ourselves to the insights and impulses which arise out of our deep inner reservoir of wisdom, dynamism and life. For if we are to be led by the Spirit of God into the land of wholeness all the energies of our being will eventually be needed to complete the journey. These imprisoned fires and underground torrents would be altogether too much for us if we had not attained some degree of strength. As was stated earlier there is no question of mastering these giant forces. We can only rule them by becoming their intelligent servants and executive agents. So we learn to live and think and work as agents of powers stronger than us, powers which are themselves created, guided and ruled by God. St Paul is describing this experience when he writes: 'I am crucified with Christ: nevertheless I live; yet not I, but Christ liveth in me.'[4] St Paul feels himself no longer the ruler of his kingdom; his old style of living has come to an end, another is in charge of his life. But at the same time he is alive as never before and, further, his obedience to the divine guide within him brings such unity and concord into his whole being that he finds himself gloriously free. This experience of life through death, and freedom through obedience, takes us out

[4] Galatians 2.20 (A.V.).

of the realm of the cardinal virtues into that of friendship with God and the inner fountain of love which makes this possible. Love, which is the fruit and the sign of the Spirit's indwelling, is the proper clothing of man; only when love has become both his inner and outer clothing is man truly 'well drest'. The cardinal virtues are subordinate, they are love's indispensable servants and helpers.

8

He That Doth Me Feed:

THE SPIRITUAL GUIDE

1

In an earlier chapter we traced the growth of heavenly love from its earliest beginnings in the clamant need-love of infants to the mature love of those who know themselves to be the friends of God, seeking God's glory, labouring for his Kingdom, gladly embracing his will. In the last two chapters we described something of the discipline without which friendship with God can be only nominal. The human journey to the land of wholeness and freedom is a step-by-step growth in heavenly love and the subsidiary strengths which love needs if it is to be genuine. That growth, the heart's pilgrimage, would be impossible without God's constant help from start to finish. This chapter's heading is taken not like all the others from George Herbert's sonnet, 'Prayer', but from his poem on the twenty-third Psalm, which speaks of God's unsleeping care under the image of a shepherd who watches over his sheep and leads them to pastures where they can find food and drink. The loving-kindness of the divine Shepherd guides and nourishes us not only through the invisible inspirations of his Spirit but through innumerable second-ary agencies. We have already referred to the child's dependence on the love, encouragement and discipline of parents and others if his humanity is to develop as it should. Indeed, though with advancing years we become less dependent on the reassurance that the regard and love of others gives, we never wholly grow out of the need of it.

There is however a special need of help for those who consciously and deliberately set out on this pilgrimage. Traditionally the aid that the pilgrim requires has been understood as spiritual direction.

The term is not wholly satisfactory, for it smacks too much of an authoritarian style of pastoral care which few Christians could endure today. We do not value obedience for its own sake as did our Christian forefathers. No doubt obedience to another when given gladly and ungrudgingly fosters humility. But obedience rendered reluctantly and with resentment hinders the development of responsibility and makes growth out of childish immaturity more difficult. In the climate of today simple, wholehearted obedience is a great deal more difficult than in the past. The director today is rather a spiritual guide than one who gives directions to be obeyed and a rule to be followed. St Teresa of Avila who took for granted the importance of a spiritual director and received much help from some of her directors tells us that she received harm from bad and ignorant directors. The true director is and always has been the Holy Spirit, and the function of a human director is to help a person to recognise where the Holy Spirit is leading him, to give him encouragement, usually much needed, and the occasional word of warning. The fear of being given authoritative advice, unsuitable to the subtleties of their own case, deters from seeking spiritual help some who would value being able to talk over their spiritual problems with an experienced person who would listen with sympathy and understanding without giving 'direction' at all.

What kind of help does the pilgrim in earnest about the journey need? At the outset he will probably need advice about prayer. It is true that we learn about prayer by praying and there is no substitute for this mode of gaining experience. Almost certainly a person who seriously decides to aim at a closer walk with God will have done a good deal of praying before ever he comes to this decision. But his prayer may be based on what he learnt as a child and may not be suitable for him any longer. There are rules and methods founded on the experience of thousands down the centuries which can prevent a person from falling into some of the pitfalls which the untaught may stumble into. The elementary grammar of prayer may be learnt from books of which there is an abundance today. But not everyone can learn from books, nor is it easy always to select from a book what is appropriate to one's own state and leave what is inappropriate. People are of very different types, and a method of prayer suitable to an extravert, who has no difficulty at all in relating to people and affairs around him but the greatest difficulty in looking within, will be unsuitable to an introvert whose problems and difficulties are precisely the opposite, and vice versa. To someone who is beginning to take the enterprise of prayer seriously it can obviously be of value to talk it over with one who is well versed in the practice and literature of prayer. A simple procedure for someone so consulted would be to invite the person to state what he actually does in prayer, how much time he gives to it, what difficulties he finds etc. The adviser can then make suggestions about the difficulties, point out ways of strengthening the prayer, perhaps suggesting a new approach to praying. There may be need of some elementary instruction on such matters as stillness, or realising God's presence, or about how to get spiritual food from reading and reflecting on the Bible, about meditation and contemplation, about the different parts of prayer – adoration and praise, confession, thanksgiving, petition and intercession. Some things are more easily caught than taught, and the spiritual guide may be able to help a person more by five or ten minutes' prayer with him at the end of an interview than by any advice given during the course of it. During this initial stage of learning to pray it is generally a help to see one's adviser regularly, perhaps every three months, to report progress or failure to progress, to mention unforeseen difficulties, to gain the encouragement which comes from the understanding and sympathy of one who is behind you in your endeavours.

Something must now be said about how to advise those who are on the threshold of contemplation or are actually embarked upon it. Should a person who is able to let his mind work passively, resting in the presence of God, be encouraged to do so and abandon what we have called expressive prayer – acts of penitence and petition, of thanksgiving, adoration and praise? The old guides assumed that contemplation was normally the climax of years of prayer and self-discipline, as a result of which a person found himself drawn increasingly to a simpler, more intuitive kind of prayer, that is to contemplation, which consists in looking and loving. Such a prayer as it develops leads to a kind of blankness in the active reasoning mind which allows or is caused by a deep Godward aspiration of the heart. Such masters of contemplation as St John of the Cross and the author of *The Cloud of Unknowing* teach that those drawn in this way should not resist the emptiness of mind but accept it as a condition of the approach to God by the way of unknowing, of loving knowledge. But there are dangers in this contemplative attitude, for passivity not only opens a person to heavenly aspirations but also to very unheavenly emotions and impulses. The old guides assumed that only those of firm faith and disciplined character could safely embark on the waters of contemplation; for only they would have the strength to cope with the powerful energies of the unconscious. A widespread contemporary problem has arisen in consequence of Eastern schools of meditation which have made a big impact in the West, especially during the past fifteen years. The best known of these schools, Transcendental Meditation, teaches a method of stilling the active mind by the repetition of a phrase in Sanscrit continuously for twenty minutes or half an hour, with the body relaxed and the attention given to the slow breathing in and out of air. This and similar methods can lead a person into the contemplative attitude, the psycho-physical state which accompanies contemplative prayer. Contemplation is more than the contemplative attitude, but can this attitude, however brought about, be a way in, perhaps a short cut, to contemplation?

I believe that for some people it is. Contemplation is a way of responding to divine grace or inspiration. All that can be taught are ways of disposing oneself to receive the grace of loving attention to God. But there can be no real contemplation for those who are not seeking to bring their whole life into harmony with God. If however this is their aim then methods such as Transcendental Meditation can help them towards this goal. But there are serious risks for those who are less than whole-hearted in their quest for oneness with God. For the mental passivity which opens a person to the grace of contemplation also leaves him open to the powerful energies of the unconscious asleep within him. The worst dangers are not, I think, those of being carried away by unbridled sensuality or aggressiveness, for the Christian will recognise these as spiritual dangers and will be warned that there is something wrong. A greater danger is the sense of discouragement which may overwhelm him as he realises where he has been led, a discouragement which may tempt him to abandon interior prayer altogether. A worse danger still, I believe, is a kind of smug self-satisfaction, the recrudescence of an infantile narcissism, which blunts a person's sensitivity to the feelings and needs of others.

Much the surest test as to whether a person is on the right lines in his prayer is the effect of his prayer in his daily life. Loving attention to God in prayer will issue in a loving concern for others and a growing indifference to a person's own wishes and interests. If there are no signs of this there must be some doubt as to the genuineness of the prayer. What advice can be given to one who is in doubt about the reality of his contemplation? It may be that I can perceive signs of a growing love and humility which the person himself cannot, and I can be reassuring. But suppose I do not see these signs and suspect that the person's doubts are justified, what advice can I offer? I can only offer tentative suggestions, for people vary greatly. I should encourage the individual to seek ways of actively thinking about God, Christ and spiritual truths and of the world in the light of these invisible realities. One way of doing this would be by reading and reflecting on the gospels and the psalms. A method I recommend is to read a short passage from a gospel, write out a prayer based on it and then pray the prayer over a number of times. I would further recommend such a person to reduce the time he gives to interior prayer to no more than twenty minutes in one session. I would further recommend him to vary the mantras he uses, having two or three for a twenty-minute period of prayer. But perhaps the greatest help one can give is to enable him to see more clearly the nature of his problem.

2

Prayer plays such an important part in the spiritual journey that usually it will be the first matter that the spiritual guide will concern himself with in those who seek his help. The journey is a pilgrimage of the heart, it is a turning of the desires more and more towards God; and this movement of desire is the very essence of prayer. But prayer ought to infuse the whole of life with its Godward orientation and if the spirit of prayer fails to colour all that a person does, then those uninfluenced aims and actions will tend to weaken the force of prayer. A person concerned to grow more at one with God will need to review his manner of life and correct whatever is at odds with this aim. Otherwise he will be like a man driving uphill with all his brakes on. In the endeavour to order our life so as to help and not hinder the Godward journey, the advice of another can be of the greatest help. In my enthusiasm for the pilgrimage I may set off at a pace which an experienced guide will know that I cannot possibly keep up. By attempting too much I court certain failure and perhaps an unpleasant tumble into the Slough of Despond. On the other hand while keen on certain particular duties or pious practices I may be oblivious of duties in other directions and need a reminder of what I am forgetting. Again there are those who believe they are committed to the spiritual journey but are not prepared to deny themselves anything. St Teresa remarked of such people that she supposed that if they avoided grave sin they would get to heaven eventually, but 'it is the pace of a hen'. Such persons may need a sharp reminder.

There are two matters which a person concerned to grow into closer union with God will need to think out carefully, matters on which advice would in most cases be helpful; the question of vocation and that of the ordering of time. Both these matters are dealt with in Chapter six but some further reflections from the point of view of one whose guidance is sought are in place here. Some persons who are sure that God is calling them to work for the Kingdom or just for people, are restless to make a quick decision and need to be warned to look before they leap. A person may rightly believe that he is being called by God without being in a position to recognise yet what precisely he is being summoned to do. For example a business executive may believe that he should give up his job and do some work which would involve him more directly in helping people, possibly in one of the caring professions. He wants to commit himself by making some decision. But it may be that the wise course is to postpone a final decision and decide instead to spend what time he can spare during the next six months in looking into various possibilities, to find out what he would be qualified to do, to investigate training schemes, to consult with people actually engaged in the work he feels drawn to. The effect of his six months of exploration could be to make him see that he should try to serve God and his fellows in his present job. On the other hand if he is still clear that he ought to make a change his decision will be a much stronger one than before because it will be far better informed. Another person in a similar position, but temperamentally different, instead of being in a hurry to make a decision is afraid to commit himself until the road before him is clear beyond a shadow of doubt. It could be that precisely the same advice would be appropriate for him as for the other but for the opposite reason. By a decision to spend six months investigating possibilities he takes positive action in the course of which the right road for him may be made plain. To seek for divine guidance does not mean doing nothing until God's will has become crystal clear. We learn both by doing and by making mistakes, and God continually guides men and women in one or both of these ways.

In the ordering of time one of the first considerations is to get priorities right. Something was said about this in Chapter six. Here certain points of importance will be mentioned or underlined. In Chapter six reference was made to living in the present moment with the mind concentrated there, undistracted by past failure or hopes and fears about the future. If this kind of relaxed concentration is to be possible hurry must be avoided. 'More haste less speed' says the proverb; speed demands concentration, haste implies the scattering of attention over many things. A certain spaciousness should be provided for in the ordering of one's time, an allotting of a little more time than is strictly necessary for the things to be done so as to leave space for recollecting what life is about. It is a common mistake of those committed to the following of Christ to do too much, to fill their day so full as to make the stillness essential for deep prayer impossible. Such people would be wise to prune their activities. The effect would be to raise the quality of what they do; and in the pilgrimage towards wholeness quality counts for much more than sheer amount. But it is difficult to cut down activities which others have come to expect of us, and we may need the reassurance that an impartial adviser can give to be able to do this with a good conscience.

In the earlier chapter reference was made to the practice of spending a few minutes daily in thinking and praying over the coming day's agenda. Over and above this some rule of life, if it is not too rigid and inflexible, can be of great value in helping a person to make sure that duties and practices of devotion are not forgotten or squeezed out. Such a rule might cover the practice of prayer, spiritual reading, meditation and contemplation, corporate worship, alms-giving and some exercise of self-examination and confession designed to strengthen repentence. Other matters of importance that might be forgotten may also be usefully incorporated into the rule. A rule of life is a means to an end. As we grow we change, and practices which once were of value cease to help us. So a rule of life unless it is extremely general needs regular revision. The body is the intimate companion and should be the ally of the soul. Reasonable care for the health of the body is a spiritual duty often neglected; and some need to be reminded to take proper exercise and enough sleep. People vary greatly in the amount of sleep they require, but enough sleep is important for spiritual as well as bodily health; the same is true of recreation – with the proviso that it is of a kind to re-create. Most of those committed to the Christian way have at least some unwritten code or mental guidelines; it can give greater strength to their commitment if they give these unwritten rules precision by writing them down. Some are helped more by an ideal which they seldom if ever are able to live up to but which continually beckons them on; others by a more modest rule which they can and do keep, except in times of rare emergency, but which they regard as a minimum and which they normally exceed. Practice alone can prove which is the better method for a particular individual.

One of the problems of giving spiritual advice is the immense variety of human beings and their diverse needs and, further, the different needs of the same person at different periods of his life. It is possible to suggest rough and ready rules which are useful provided that it is realised that exceptional circumstances make exceptions to rule wholly legitimate. In general it can be said that prayer should be related to a person's life situation and as the situation varies so should the prayer. Children above all need the security provided by parents and a good home. In adolescence and early adulthood the need is to break out of the parent-dominated world of childhood, to strike out on their own, to get settled in a job or career, to marry and make a home of their own or, possibly, to embrace a vocation which excludes marriage or excludes it for a time. In middle life it is important to come to terms with elements within themselves which were perforce suppressed or not allowed to develop at a time when most of their energies had to be given to launching themselves in a job or career and building a home. Middle life is the time when all need to grow in self-knowledge. It would be generally true to say that children should be encouraged to realise God as their heavenly Father, loving them, watching over them, guiding them. In adolescence and early adulthood devotion should be encouraged to fasten on to the figure of the Lord Jesus Christ, the Pioneer of salvation, and his call to discipleship and the risks which that entails. In middle life a person is likely to be drawn to a more interior religion and should be helped to recognise the presence of the Holy Spirit guiding him from within his own heart and mind.

Metanoia, the redirection of heart and mind which the following of Christ demands, is not a once-for-all happening. Though it may have its decisive moments it is an attitude which needs to grow. In fact spiritual growth might be described as growth in *metanoia*, an increasing turning of the whole person towards God and away from whatever is opposed to the Godward orientation. *Metanoia* will be different for the boy or girl and for the adult. For the young, repentance will generally mean the deliberate embracing of a Christ-inspired ideal and the striving to be true to it. It will include the expression of penitence and self-blame for failure to live up to the ideal. It is important that those who guide the young should endeavour, without damping the enthusiasm of youth, to temper it with realism. No doubt we learn much from failure and the young must be allowed this method of growing wiser. But to attempt impossibilities will be to make failure inevitable and the discouragement which is bound to follow. Later on in life *metanoia* will mean something rather different; it will consist primarily in the search for deeper self-awareness and self-acceptance. Whereas the young generally need encouragement to persevere in their efforts to follow Christ and live true to their ideal, older men and women more often need to be encouraged to stop trying harder and to learn to trust more. Instead of blaming themselves for their repeated and sickening failure to live up to their ideal they should search for the inner causes of their failure. As self-awareness grows the ideal itself must be enlarged to allow within its scope interests and activities which previously it had excluded. Together with a stronger commitment to God there should come about a greater tolerance of the uncertainties and mysteries of life, a greater willingness to live with questions to which there is no simple answer, a greater reluctance to pass judgement on others whose beliefs and manner of life are markedly different from their own.

A great deal of guidance is given by the clergy in the course of hearing confessions. Those who habitually make use of the sacrament of absolution may expect to receive advice there and may be reluctant to receive it outside that context. But there are disadvantages in giving spiritual guidance during the administering of this sacrament. For such guidance should be concerned about the whole of a person's life, whereas the primary matter of confession is that tiny fraction of his life which is his actual sins. Spiritual guidance can usually be much better given in the relaxed atmosphere of a talk. There is growing up a practice of combining spiritual guidance with the sacrament of absolution by first talking over things in a study or some other convenient room and then, if need be, for the person to go on, perhaps quite informally, to make some specific act of confession and to receive absolution. But the ministry of the sacrament of absolution needs fuller consideration, which it will receive in the next chapter. We must now turn from considering the kind of advice a spiritual director might give to his whole approach to the task and to the persons who come to him for guidance.

3

It is of the utmost importance, I believe, to regard all those who come for spiritual counsel with a deep and sensitive respect. Each individual is unique, he is a profound mystery, an unknown country which we can only hope to explore by listening and reflecting, by asking the questions which draw a person out and make it easy for him to speak. People are more important than their problems and people are never easy to understand in any depth. Sometimes a problem is unfolded that seems relatively simple and a quick answer might be made which from the abstract point of view would be correct. But it may be wise not to be in a hurry to offer the answer. The problem may be simple but the person is not, and a quick confident answer may send the person away dissatisfied and feeling he was a fool to have troubled us. I believe we prefer to meet some perplexity in our counsellors rather than too easy a comprehension.

The sensitive respect which we owe to all men is especially important towards those who approach us for the first time. An individual may come feeling nervous and afraid of what we may think of him. How freely he may feel able to speak about some humiliating personal problem or domestic dispute will much depend on the impression he forms of us. He who would guide others must learn to listen well to what they say. This may be difficult for those, such as the clergy, who have frequently to play the role of teacher. It is important to keep silent and not normally to interrupt, except in order to ask a question to elucidate or amplify some obscure or

enigmatic remark or, occasionally, to bring back to the point someone who has strayed away from it for too long. Sometimes it may
be necessary to pull up someone who is making the interview an
excuse for a tirade against another or against a whole class of
persons. It may also happen that a person ostensibly seeking guidance is really trying to enlist our support in some quarrel or dispute
and we may have to reply in the spirit of Jesus' saying: 'Who made
me a judge or divider over you?'[1] But such cases are the exception.
In general the rule, 'silence is golden', is the right one for those who
have to counsel others.

Often I am tempted when listening to some distressing story to
interrupt with a reassuring remark. 'Surely things can't be quite so
bad as that?' or 'I am sure that everything will come right eventually.' Such remarks may be right at the end, after we have listened
a long time and have asked questions to elucidate the trouble, but
as interruptions they may be felt as attempts to change the subject,
as a refusal to listen. Indeed our reassuring remarks are sometimes
made to reassure ourselves and protect our feelings from being
further harrowed. Occasionally a person will seek guidance in order,
perhaps without realising it, to escape the responsibility of decision.
Our function is to help people to make their own decisions as wisely
and responsibly as possible, not to make their decisions for them.
In the long run it may be better that a person make a mistake
through acting according to his own best judgement than to avoid
it by following the judgement of another. There are many morally
dubious situations, especially where a person is confronted with a
choice of evils, in which the most helpful way of giving advice would
be to ask him what he himself believed to be best and then give
qualified approval in some such words as 'that may well be the
right course'.

The function of the spiritual guide differs from but overlaps that
of the professional counsellor, whether social case worker or psychotherapist. He can learn much of value in his own task from the
experience and skills of the counselling professions, especially in the
art of listening. I mention three qualities which have been found
important in the work of counselling. The first of these is empathy.
Empathy is something more than sympathy. It is partly the ability
to enter into a kind of emotional rapport with another person so

[1] Luke 12.14.

that one's emotions vibrate in harmony with his. Babies commonly have this rapport with their mothers and animals sometimes have it with their masters. It is partly also the ability to enter imaginatively into the situation and the feelings of another, to put oneself in his shoes. Persons vary in their ability to empathise but by effort and training the ability can be greatly developed. It is important to listen not only to the words spoken but to the tone of voice, to the signs of emotion, or strain, or pain which the words may partly conceal but which an attentive ear may pick up. An obstacle to listening in depth, listening to the emotions behind the words, is an insufficient awareness of our own emotions. It is common for those who value clear thinking, intellectuals in general, to repress their feelings, which get in the way of accurate thought. Inattention to his own feelings is often encouraged by the thinker partly so as not to be distracted from seemingly more important matters, but partly from fear of being carried away into an embarrassing display of emotion. If my feelings are deeply repressed I shall either be totally unable to empathise and will find listening extremely boring or I shall empathise too much; my feelings will carry me away and I shall embarrass myself without being able to help my client. A good test of the ability to empathise with someone in need of guidance is the ability to put in our own words the problem or difficulty which he is struggling incoherently to articulate. If the person whose help I am seeking is able to put clearly in his own words the worry or the pain which I can only murmur about in a confused and muddled manner, then I know that I am understood and that it will be safe to say more about my troubles.

A second quality important for establishing a good relationship between a counsellor and his client is what has been called genuineness or truthfulness about our feelings. People who are strictly veracious about matters of fact will often lie outrageously about their feelings. I am not thinking of the person who displays all the tell-tale signs of anger and then denies that he is angry. It is possible that he is unaware of the anger which is so patent to everyone else and so is not telling a deliberate lie. Some people are so out of touch with their feelings as sometimes to be unaware of powerful emotions, which they are likely to project on to someone else. What I have in mind is the deliberate pretending to be pleased when we are not or not to mind some wounding remark when in fact we are badly hurt. On ordinary social occasions most people find it necessary sometimes to dissemble their real feelings so as to avoid giving pain. There are polite lies which deceive nobody. Again, a mother on the eve of a children's party over which she must preside receives some bad news which makes her feel thoroughly cast down. But she forces herself to maintain a smiling face, so far as she can, so as not spread gloom over the party. But in the context of counselling where a trusting relation between counsellor and client is of great importance untruthfulness about what we feel is a blunder. For a good relationship is formed and maintained chiefly on the level of feeling; and such a relationship is impossible with someone who conceals his feelings behind a polite mask. Perhaps the principle of genuineness about our feelings is most usefully applied in its negative form of never saying anything which contradicts what you feel deep down. If I am hurt by a sneering remark about myself or a friend of mine I may decide that it would be too damaging to say straight out what I feel (though sometimes this might be right) but at least I will not try to smile as though I were indifferent to it; instead I will say nothing. When I am angered by some thinly veiled insult, I may feel it wise not to respond with an indignant verbal attack but I will not pretend to be impervious to attack. At such a time the habit of being slow to speak is invaluable. From all this it is clear that if we are to give guidance to others we need to make ourselves aware of our own feelings. Self-awareness is essential not only for the knowledge of God but for any deep understanding of our fellows.

The third of the qualities required for good counselling has been called non-possessive warmth. Paul Halmos, a sociologist, in his book about the counselling profession, *The Faith of the Counsellors*[2], argues that the success or failure of professional counsellors depends far more on their ability to communicate a sense of caring love than on the particular psychological theories they hold. As the warmth of the sun causes the seed to germinate in the soil so the warmth of human kindness enables people to become less anxious, to relax, to grow. But it is easy for affection to grow possessive and so to hinder the growth of a person which at first it had helped. The psychoanalysts warn us of the phenomenon of the transference and also of the counter-transference. The patient under analysis finds that the buried feelings of dependence, which as a child he felt towards his

[2] Constable 1965.

parents, on being made conscious attach themselves irresistibly to the analyst, so that he feels towards the analyst the same affection and need to be loved which as a child he felt towards his father or mother. But the analyst also is liable to find that the patient's need for his love calls out strong parental feelings towards him. Should the analyst lack sufficient self-awareness he may find himself as compulsively attached to his patient as the patient is to him. This is one reason why analysts before they are authorised to practise are required to undergo a training analysis. For analysis is one of the ways in which a person can be helped to become aware of his buried emotions. Something analogous to the transference and counter-transference is likely to occur in all close relationships where one person seeks help from another, though it will be weaker than in the exceptionally intimate relationship between analyst and patient. Most of those who have had the experience of listening to someone pouring out his troubles to them will know the feeling of warmth which springs up and the desire to protect and comfort which is typical of parental love. It is important for us to recognise this and to take care not to allow this affection to spoil our judgement and to lose sight of the real interests of those who seek our help. I need to be ruthless with my feelings when they are in danger of hindering the growth of another's proper independence.

An Arab story makes a picturesque parable of this quality of non-possessive warmth. A certain Arab had three sons to whom he bequeathed in his will all his wealth in the following proportions. The eldest was to have half, the second a third and the youngest a ninth. When he died his wealth was found to consist of seventeen camels. The sons in perplexity as to how to effect a division of this awkward number asked the advice of an old Arab, a friend of the family. He said to them, 'I have a camel which I don't need, take him and you will be able to make your division.' They accepted the camel and proceeded to calculate the division. One half of eighteen is nine, a third is six, a ninth is two. Nine plus six plus two make seventeen. They had one camel over which they gratefully returned to the old Arab. The counsellor has to be like the eighteenth camel. He may be essential to a person in solving a problem or facing a crisis. But having given his help he should withdraw in order to allow the person to be free of dependence on him.

The three qualities, empathy, genuineness and non-possessive warmth are closely linked. Each of them demands self-awareness, more particularly awareness of our deep feelings. This is necessary if we are to listen with patience and sympathetic understanding to the distresses of our fellows. For if we are unconscious of our feelings the troubles poured into our ears will awaken anxiety or fear or revulsion or anger by stirring up deep within us the sleeping dogs which we have been ignoring.

4

There are of course important differences between the aim of the spiritual guide and that of the professional counsellor. The spiritual guide seeks to help a person to grow into a deeper and more committed relationship to God, while the professional counsellor is concerned to help him to cope better with his human relationships. He is dealing for the most part with persons undergoing an emotional crisis whether due to inner problems or hostile circumstances. The spiritual guide, on the other hand, gives continuous support and advice whether the person who seeks his help is undergoing exceptional stress or not. But despite the differences there is some overlap between the two disciplines. For those looking for spiritual guidance live in the same world and are subject to the same crises as those who seek psychotherapy. The spiritual must not be divorced from the natural. Rather the two spheres interpenetrate and influence each other. Grace heals and perfects nature which should be the Spirit's ally on the Godward journey. But nature despised or ignored can frustrate the work of grace. Bad human relationships are an obstacle to union with God and circumstances can be so harsh as to crush the spirits of all but the strongest. The spiritual director should encourage those who need it to seek psychiatric help and should regard the psychotherapist as an ally not a rival. But his relationship with those who seek his guidance is likely to be indirectly therapeutic. Certainly he should seek to acquire and develop the qualities of empathy, genuineness and non-possessive warmth and to seek to grow in the self-awareness which is important for all close relationships.

What other qualities are needed by the spiritual guide? It would be possible to compile such a list of desirable qualities as would deter anyone with the least scrap of modesty from venturing to undertake an office which demands sanctity, learning and supernatural powers of discernment. But in fact people do not set themselves up as spiritual guides as a doctor might put up a brass plate outside his house to tell the public of his availability. For the most part they are pressed into the position by those who discern in them the qualities of insight and sympathy that they desire in a guide of souls. Father Somerset Ward, the best-known Anglican director of this century, was persuaded to give up more and more of his time to this work by people who having attended a retreat conducted by him asked him to become their spiritual father, or soul friend, to use the phrase which Kenneth Leech has brought into currency again. To a lesser degree, I believe, this has been the experience of all those who have become known as spiritual directors. Instead of listing the qualities of the ideal guide of souls I propose to name certain mimimum qualifications without which no one ought to accept the responsibility of guiding another, and then to suggest ways in which a person might equip himself further for this task.

No one should undertake to guide others on the spiritual journey who is not himself deeply committed to it. Further he should be interested in the theory and practice of the spiritual life. For people vary and one man's path will follow a different route from another's. Without some knowledge of ways other than his own he may lead other people astray. Having said this it is necessary to add that he should have found some spiritual method which has proved of value to himself. One who is a jack of all trades and master of none should not undertake to guide others. Over and above his concern for the spiritual journey he should have a caring love for people and a genuine concern for their spiritual well-being. These minimum qualifications are possessed not only by many of the clergy but also by many lay people. Most of those who have become well known as spiritual directors have been priests, but there have been noted directors among the laity, some of them women. Baron von Hügel and Evelyn Underhill spring to mind among the spiritual guides of this century. I have spoken of minimum qualifications not because I regard them as sufficient but because as with other skills we learn by doing. There is no substitute for experience; but everyone is short of experience to begin with; and a start must be made with inadequate knowledge if it is to be made at all.

How does a person who possesses these minimum qualifications face the task of giving guidance to someone who seeks his help? He will remember that the Holy Spirit is the true guide; he will listen to what the person says, perhaps ask him questions to draw him out, ask him how he believes he is being led and urge him to pray to the Holy Spirit for further guidance. Probably he will say a word or two of encouragement, possibly a word of caution. But I believe that usually the less said the better and that as a rule we help more by prayer together for wisdom and strength than by advice. But whether or not we pray in the interview, to undertake the responsibility of acting as spiritual guide to someone is to assume an obligation to pray on his behalf, both for him and for light from God about him.

What will equip the spiritual guide for his work more than anything is his own persevering prayer and his own personal struggle with the forces of darkness, and his effort to bring under the sway of the Spirit the untamed energies of his own being. The study of the Christian tradition of the spiritual life, especially the acknowledged masters of prayer, will enlarge the store of wisdom from which he can draw.[3] The study of modern psychology will help to provide a contemporary language which makes ancient wisdom bright and new. But in the understanding of others, I believe, psychology helps most indirectly. Its primary use for the spiritual guide is to help him to a greater self-awareness. This enlarged knowledge of himself and of his weakness, his vulnerability and his dependence on divine grace will enable him to enter intuitively into an understanding of others and their trials. The distresses of others will awaken echoes in his own soul, he has been there before or near there, his own remembered affliction will enable him to speak words of strength and reassurance.

---

[3] *Soul Friend*, Kenneth Leech, Sheldon Press 1977. This gives an excellent history of spiritual direction. There is a useful Select Bibliography in the appendix.

9

The Soul's Blood:

MAN'S HEALING AND LIBERATION

1

In the last chapter we considered the function of the spiritual guide as that of helping men and women to recognise and follow where the Spirit is leading them. In this chapter I want to reflect on and around one particular part of the spiritual guide's task, receiving the confessions of his fellows and ministering absolution. A great deal of rethinking concerning this ministry of reconciliation has been going on during the past fifty years. And before this means of grace can be seen in its right context, some misunderstandings and false emphases both of theory and practice need to be cleared away and some old truths recalled. I begin by reflecting on some of the rich metaphors of George Herbert's poem.

This poem though ostensibly about prayer is at the same time a meditation on the work of man's salvation. There is nothing artificial or contrived in placing prayer in the setting of redemption. For the Christian's prayer is in part a response to God's self-disclosure in Jesus Christ and the recalling of this and its consequences is the normal context of his praying. The most immediate association of blood for Herbert was, in all probability, life; for the Old Testament identifies the mysterious quality which distinguishes a living from a dead being with blood. Prayer is the soul's life blood; without prayer it must die. The vast increase since biblical times in our knowledge of the physiology of the human body in no way destroys the power of the symbol. For the circulation of the blood, unknown to the Hebrews, maintains the life of the body, both by distributing the nourishing energy derived from food and drink and air to each part of the body, and by carrying away the waste and the impurities.

But 'the soul's blood' also speaks to the Christian of the blood of Christ, shed on the cross, expiating sin and ending, in principle, the alienation caused by the fall. Prayer is a sharing in what was undergone on the cross. It is 'Christ-side-piercing spear'. Perhaps this means that prayer is a spear that pierces the side of Christ and draws from it the healing stream of blood and water. The words hint at the double stream which speaks of God's love cleansing us in the waters of baptism and renewing us in the eucharist. It also calls to mind some words from another of Herbert's poems: 'Love is that liquor sweet and most divine/Which my God feels as blood and I as wine.'[1] Prayer is the voice of the Spirit through whose circulating energy the whole person is renewed; the voice of the Spirit who awakens aspirations of love and longing towards our true goal, who presses us to accept and live out our humanity to the utmost of our capacity, with something of the generosity and courage with which Jesus lived. It is the especial work of the Spirit to identify us with Christ, the eternal Word of God and especially with that point in time when the Word spoke most resoundingly, the death on the cross. This identification is spelt out ritually in the twin sacraments of baptism and the eucharist. 'So many of us as were baptised into Jesus Christ were baptised into his death.'[2] 'As often as you eat this bread and drink the cup you proclaim the Lord's death until he comes.'[3] But this continually renewed sacramental identification with the death of Christ has to be lived out in the work and play, the love and companionship, the struggle and stress, the failures and the falling short of daily life. This is the context of the sacrament of absolution, which is a further means by which we are brought back to the rock from whence we were hewn, the crucified Son of God.

Before however we examine the meaning of this powerful sacrament of healing and liberation, let us look at the life of man from the perspective of Christ's death and resurrection. For the life through death which the Christian believes he has received reminds us that in the world of nature death is the indispensable servant of life. The pattern of life through death is spread out on the vast canvas of creation. The death of winter is the necessary prelude to

[1] From *The Agonie* by George Herbert.
[2] Romans 6.3 (A.V.).
[3] 1 Corinthians 11.26.

the burst of new life in the spring. The human body reconstitutes itself every seven years by the death of every particle of it so that it may be renewed by the birth of fresh cells. Physical death is something passive, something which happens to us. We shall be forced when our time comes to relinquish our possessions, to lose control of our bodily being, to let go of physical life. There is a kind of dying which is a necessary part of healthy life and growth, a letting go of the past in order to face and grasp the demands of the present and the future. The child undergoes a little death when he goes to school for the first time, leaving the security of the home and facing the strange and seemingly threatening world of the school. The boy or girl undergoes a kind of death when, on leaving school and letting go of that now familiar world, he enters the new world of work and of earning a living or possibly the uncertainty and the demoralising frustration of unemployment. In happy circumstances the series of little deaths which are part and parcel of growing up, can be welcomed with zest as the prelude to a new and exciting life in a larger and more interesting world. But this letting go of past securities is given a sinister colouring of fear and foreboding by the harsh fact of human selfishness, arrogance and cruelty, by the reality of our estrangement from our Maker, from our fellows and from our own true being. Ideally, the succession of little deaths which meet us from the cradle to the grave, which we must undergo if we are to find fulfilment, can be met cheerfully in hope of what lies ahead and without backward glances. But owing to our condition of estrangement we tend to cling tenaciously to the old and to face the new with reluctance and misgiving. We dread the loss of old security and of finding ourselves vulnerable. To overcome our dread our Author has come among us as a man among men, and as a man endured that dread at its extreme worst in order to break its power and rescue from its tyranny all who will trust themselves to him.

The divine-human deed on the cross of Calvary is both a fact of the past and a power in the present. The cross, together with the resurrection which established its meaning, launched the body of believers, the Christian Church, on its voyage down the centuries. The cross sheds a brilliant light on the character of the Creator which is transforming (all too slowly) the way Christians reflect upon him and worship him. The cross is the master key to unlock the dungeon doors of fear and rage, of greed and lust and despair which hold men and women imprisoned. It is a tree of healing, alive and growing within the brotherhood of believers, whose leaves bring health to the sick in mind and balm to the sorrowing. It is an elixir of fire and force to rouse the hearts and strengthen the arms of those who do battle for justice and right. Above all it is the climax of the strategy of Love almighty which St Paul has summed up in the terse sentence, 'God was in Christ reconciling the world to himself.'[4]

I have found it necessary to meditate at some length on the mystery of the cross in order to put the sacrament of absolution in its proper context. For there is a real danger of its being trivialised by routine and then dismissed as an irrelevance. There is also the opposite danger of its being shunned through misunderstanding of its place in the economy of grace and its intimate connection with the reconciling cross. The Christian ministry is a ministry of reconciliation and a branch growing out of the tree of healing. The protest is sometimes heard: 'I don't want anyone to come between my soul and God.' Behind such words as these lies the right and proper sense that our approach to God should be direct and personal, that we should have free access to our Maker. But the words fail to take into account the fact that God's love to which we are responding when we approach him is largely mediated by others, beginning in the first hours of our life when our mothers and others acted as the agents of God. The gospel is entrusted to human beings who, despite their human defects, mediate the good news to others. St Paul speaks of God as entrusting to his servants the message of reconciliation: 'We are ambassadors for Christ, God making his appeal through us.'[5] Reconciliation, the breaking down of the barriers which estrange men from God is a function of the whole Church. The whole Church is meant to be a reconciling body, mediating the love of God both to its own members and to those outside it and on its fringes. The priest is set apart especially for this task of mediation. He fulfils it in many ways, through preaching and teaching, through listening and giving advice, through a variety of social encounters and relationships. He is, however unworthy and inadequate, both the agent of Christ and the representative of the Church. This is especially true when he celebrates the sacra-

[4] 2 Corinthians 5.19.
[5] 2 Corinthians 5.20.

ments of baptism and the eucharist. The sacrament of absolution is another part of this mediating ministry in which he acts in the name of God and as the voice of the Church.

The power of the sacrament to liberate and heal is partly due to the fact that it links the penitent believer with his fellow-members of Christ's Body. The sin which estranges us from God estranges us from our fellows and it is, therefore, fitting that our reconciliation should be brought about through the ministry of one who acts as the representative of the Church, or, to put it more precisely, as the representative of Christ in the Church. The consciousness of having a direct and personal access to God, right and true though it is, can sometimes make us feel independent of our fellows, which is an error. Receiving forgiveness through the sacramental channel without destroying the personal nature of our approach to God brings home our dependence on our fellows in the Church of God.

Another reason for the power of the sacrament is its symbolic resonance. This symbolic character enables it to reach and resound in areas of our being which are outside our control and perhaps outside our awareness. It is as though deep within us there lives a child, the child which we once were, subject to uncontrollable moods of fear and anxiety, of resentment and self-pity and despair. The childish thing in us is impervious to the reasoning which satisfies our sophisticated adult consciousness but is open to the power of symbols. My reason tells me that if I repent God forgives, but this does not necessarily satisfy the anxious child within. Am I sure that my repentance is genuine? So there is that in me which rejoices to hear the voice of one who speaks with the authority of Christ in his Church assuring me that I am forgiven: 'By his authority committed unto me I absolve thee from all thy sin.'

The peace and reassurance which sacramental absolution normally brings is made possible because it has been preceded by a true and honest confession of sin. Again it is the child in us especially that needs to make a simple and unsophisticated acknowledgement of the things done amiss or left undone. Children can be made miserable by some unconfessed misdemeanour and are enormously relieved when they have confessed it. So too the child in us is glad when we have confessed our sins, however embarrassed our sophisticated selves may feel. Further, though in form confession is an act by which we impart information, its importance comes much more from its being a means of expressing, and so of strengthening, repentance, our turning to God and away from what is against God. The realisation that God knows all and needs no information from us about our fallings short can make any detailed confession in private seem unreal. But repentance if genuine must of necessity concern itself with the concrete and the detailed and not merely with generalities. For this reason confession before another, who does not know beforehand what we are going to say, brings a bracing realism into this act of repentance.

2

Many who wholeheartedly accept the truth of these considerations for those who have fallen into grave sin are uneasy at the use of the sacrament of absolution as a normal part of the Christian life. Their misgivings deserve to be looked at squarely, for I believe they may point to a new and unrealised power in the sacrament for the healing and liberation of men and women. The original use of the sacrament was for the absolution of those who had fallen into grave sin, such as murder, adultery, robbery or the denial of the faith to save one's life, sins grave enough to cause public scandal. The extension of the sacrament to the absolution of those guilty of comparatively minor sins of which few are innocent has in the course of time changed the use of the sacrament. It is true that according to Church canon law, which dates from the year 1215 and has never been changed, only grave sins need to be absolved sacramentally. But the practice of confessions of devotion, in which minor fallings short are confessed, has spread until the original use has been obscured. What is disturbing about this is not that a person should confess and be absolved from the bad language he used under provocation or the catty remark he passed on some acquaintance, but the sense that such sins are only the tip of the iceberg; they are symptoms of something much more profoundly wrong, of an estrangement from God, of a state of sin; and the absolution which sets the conscience at rest about the minor sins leaves this sinfulness untouched. For we cannot be content to include only what is free and to some extent a deliberate act under the heading of sin. We must also include the profound fear, anxiety, anger, resentment, depression, partly conscious, partly unconscious as within sin's domain. For these powerful and usually unwanted

emotions are the seed bed of wrong actions, they are part of the
kingdom of Satan from which Christ came to deliver us. The sacrament of absolution must of course remain as the means by which
those whose consciences are burdened with grave sin can gain
pardon and peace. But I believe it should be extended to become
increasingly also the sacrament of healing and deliverance by means
of which our moral sicknesses are cured and the chains of habit,
which hamper our freedom and prevent us from acting as we would
and should, are broken.

If this extension of the use of the sacrament of absolution is to be
made there will need to be some change in our attitude to the act
of confession itself. The actual sins which by long-standing custom
we confess are acts, or failures to act, for which we know ourselves
to blame and deliberately acknowledge that we are to blame: the
deliberate evasion of some duty, the face-saving lie, the piece of
dishonesty, the contemptuous remark. By so acknowledging my
responsibility I affirm my dignity as a free man and strengthen my
determination to act responsibly for the future. But there is that
whole underworld of bad and unhealthy emotion, referred to above,
which willy-nilly corrupts my intentions and weakens my best
resolves. I cannot help this by any effort of will. It is not something
for which I can realistically blame myself, though it is undoubtedly
bad and hinders my growth in love for God and my neighbour. I
believe that so far as I am aware of these unwholesome emotions
and impulses I should confess them, but in a wholly different manner from that in which I acknowledge my sinful acts.

Just as it is right and wholesome to blame myself for the wrong
actions which I deliberately did or the right actions which I wrongly
left undone, to blame myself for the painful mood of depression or
acute anxiety which sweeps over me, which I cannot help and do
not want, is likely to make bad worse and throw me into one of
Giant Despair's dungeons. Yet these moods are bad and I believe
should be acknowledged. Perhaps the distinction between two
meanings of responsibility can indicate two essentially different
emphases in my acknowledgement of my estrangement from God.
I confess my responsibility in one way when I say 'I have sinned
through my own fault'; I am saying that I am to blame. That is
one sense of responsibility. But if during a war a naval officer takes
over the command of a ship which has been damaged by enemy
action he is not to blame for the condition of the ship when he

assumed command, but from that point on he is responsible for doing all he can to make good the damage and to exercise his command wisely. This is the other sense of responsibility. Most of us when we reach years of discretion are hampered by bad habits which we developed in response to frightening or seductive experiences when we were much younger. We are not to blame or only very slightly for this unfortunate legacy from the past, but we are responsible for doing our best to overcome or perhaps get cured of our bad tendencies or at least for learning to manage them responsibly. It is often in practice impossible to draw a line between the failures I know I am to blame for and those which probably I could not have helped. But I believe the distinction is true and important and to bear it in mind makes for reality in our approach to God.

It is because of the need to acknowledge the evil that I cannot, or feel that I cannot, help that I welcome the tendency to link confession and absolution with informal conversation in a more relaxed atmosphere than is possible or proper when a person kneels before the crucifix in the confessional. If I confess only the actual sins I can remember I may have very little to say and what I do say may seem trivial. For all the time I am aware of something far more profoundly wrong than the little selfishnesses that I acknowledge. There is no deep repentence, no whole-hearted turning to God, large areas of my being are uninvolved in my repentance. And yet this uncommitted part of me weighs like a heavy haversack on my shoulders and prevents my walking freely in the road along which God is calling me. What I need is not so much forgiveness from my actual sins but deliverance from this hampering weight, the cure of my soul's sickness, the dressing and the binding up of the unhealed wounds of the past. This thorough renewal of our being is what Christ came to make available and the Church is commissioned to minister.

If my soul's sickness is to be cured and the wounds of the past healed they must be acknowledged; and before they can be acknowledged they must be identified and recognised for what they are. This realisation demands searching self-examination, a difficult task which only I can carry out. But if no one can do this work for me I can be greatly helped by someone in whom I have confidence enough to trust. Solitary self-examination is liable to lead us into an emotional labyrinth whose twisting and criss-crossing passages leave us confused and lost and we are tempted to abandon in despair the quest for self-knowledge. It is safer to conduct the search in the presence of another who stands outside my particular labyrinth and can see better than I where the crooked corridors lead.

What are the kind of things I need to talk over, to expose to the light of another's gaze? Here are some of them: my anxieties and fears which my reason tells me are groundless but disturb and distract me none the less; my enmities, antagonisms, dislikes which I see to be largely irrational but cannot get rid of; my unrealistic ambitions which constantly interfere with my better judgement and lead me into foolish mistakes; my evasions and procrastinations which betray the presence of unfaced fears; my morbid guilt feelings which interfere with my whole-hearted and responsible commitment to life; my feelings of suppressed rage which are seldom if ever expressed in overt word or action but create a chilling atmosphere around me; the black moods which sap all my energy and make life seem pointless. What help can my spiritual friend give me when I have opened my heart to him and let this perilous stuff out? Or, if the position is reversed and my brother or sister comes to me for help, what can I say or do?

3

It is a cause for reassurance to recall that in this ministry we act as agents of God; we speak for God, and God acts through us. Our function is to the best of our ability to mediate God's compassion which is all the time searching for ways to heal and liberate. If the realisation of God's ceaseless love and care could penetrate into the deep places of the heart then the chains which bind us would snap and the prison doors open. It is for us to help this to happen. Somehow by what we are, by our attitude and manner and by what we say we are to be channels of this care and compassion. It is a constant astonishment to those involved in this ministry how much people are helped just by being listened to with sympathy. The love of God is made real and concrete through the human listener whether or not it is recognised as God's love. Divine love works for the most part anonymously. Many outside the ranks of the Church's ordained ministry exercise this ministry of compassionate listening and are God's agents whether they realise this or not. But though listening is perhaps the most universally valuable part of this ministry to our frail and stumbling fellow-sinners it is not the only part. We touched on this in the previous chapter. Indeed listening with compassion does not mean sitting in dumb silence while our companion talks. Often he needs much sympathetic questioning before he is able to talk at all. It may be necessary to interject questions to clarify an obscure statement or probe what lies behind an enigmatic remark. Sometimes a person is worried by some simple mistake or misunderstanding which can be quickly cleared up. Sometimes we are expected to say something and sometimes we feel obliged to say something whether or not this is expected. Sometimes I may feel repelled or disgusted by the sordid story I hear and I need to remind myself of Christ's words: 'Judge not, and you will not be judged; condemn not, and you will not be condemned.'[6] I do not condemn, partly, it may be, because of Christ's injunction, but partly also because I am too well aware how little I know of the strength of the inner compulsions and morbid cravings which are the hidden causes that drive a person into actions which he knows to be shameful. But neither do I condone the actions or say anything to weaken the person's will to seek deliverance from the compulsions which drove him to it or to undermine his sense of responsibility for doing what he can to manage and restrain them. It is all too easy with the intention of reassuring a person and quieting morbidly exaggerated guilt feelings to suggest that his actions or his state are not bad after all. This is no real service to a person struggling for freedom and may very likely undermine our influence with him and our power to help him.

What is of the greatest importance, I believe, is to assure the person of God's powerful love and compassion ceaselessly at work around him and within, bent on setting him free. This is best done, I believe, by praying with him, partly in silence, partly in short sentences of prayer which express confidence in God's powerful love and gratitude for what that love has done and is doing. If actual sins have been mentioned the prayer should include confident petition for forgiveness. If we are priests with authority to pronounce absolution this can appropriately be given here. For myself I prefer to end with the laying on of hands with prayer. The most symbolically expressive way of doing this, I think, is to place one hand on

[6] Luke: 37–8.

the forehead and the other on the back of the head, which suggests God's surrounding and protecting love.

There is a healing and liberating force in the good news of God's love and power, whether proclaimed from the pulpit or shared in a one-to-one personal encounter. But it seems that often in order to be healed we have to expose our wounds, just as when we seek medical help we declare our symptoms to the doctor before we expect him to diagnose our complaint or prescribe treatment. Many of our present weaknesses and sins are rooted in the past. They are the effects of emotional wounds received long ago which led to the formation of bad habits. These, grown strong with time, fetter our freedom in the present. If we are to be free of these chains their original cause may have to be brought to light and faced. Sometimes a person's trouble is so deep-seated that we need to recommend him to seek the help of an expert psychotherapist, who will act as the agent of God's compassion. But this help may not always be available or may be too expensive. We may have to encourage a person to endure an affliction which for the time at least cannot be cured. But there are other resources which a pastor with a little psychological knowledge can call upon. I mention one which has recently come to the fore – the healing of the memories.

Many old habits and attitudes are hard to change because they have their roots in painful experiences in the past and the memories which keep them alive. These unhappy memories secrete a kind of poison which weakens and even paralyses our goodwill. If I am to live as I should these memories which are contaminating the springs of life must be healed. Take for example over-anxiety or the feeling of being unlovable which causes me to put up barriers against the friendly approaches of others. Neither of these moods can be overcome by will-power alone. I may sometimes by an effort be able to dismiss them from my mind, but that is not the end of them. They carry on a kind of underground movement corrupting my goodwill and weakening my efforts and, sooner or later, they will push their way up into consciousness again. These unwelcome feelings, arising out of the past, are partly kept alive by memory. What I can recall is perhaps only the tip of the iceberg and what started me off on my habit of getting over-anxious may have happened in early childhood before I can remember. I find myself beginning to get anxious about some trifling matter and try to put it away. But my effort is of no avail and a flood of anxious feelings pours into my mind and

I am thoroughly worried. Or, take the feeling of self-rejection, the feeling of being unlovable. This almost certainly goes back to some painful incident or perhaps many incidents in the past when my need for affection was cruelly rebuffed. This has saddled me with two contradictory feelings, the desire to be loved and resentment at not being loved, and at the same time a protective barrier built by the fear of being rebuffed again, which fends off the approach of anyone who would offer me love. Or resentment at my loneliness makes me always liable to fits of anger. A tiny little annoyance triggers off a gust of rage, a molehill is magnified into a mountain because the small irritant is fed by a subterranean river of resentment from the past. It is the last of a long line of instances of my being unfairly treated and I explode in anger.

I have given two examples of the way in which the dead hand of the past can cripple our efforts to follow Christ in the present and can prevent our growing to our full human stature. It is possible to see these waves of over-anxiety or resentment which from time to time sweep over me as temptations which, by the grace of God, I struggle to resist. But there is another and a better possibility. It is better to drain the marshes that breed the malarial mosquito than to multiply the means of treating the disease. This better possibility is to open the old emotional wounds, together with the memories which feed the flow of poison, to the grace of Christ and the healing power of the cross. We open ourselves to Christ through believing prayer which can be greatly helped by faith-controlled imagination. Further, though it is possible to open ourselves to him in the solitude of private prayer, faith, which is all-important, can be much strengthened by the presence of another whose faith supports ours and who will pray with us. Many of those who are charged with the spiritual care of individuals are learning to help them in this way. What we have to do is to pray to Christ with confidence and to pray specifically, to ask for the healing of the particular wounds which are spoiling our life. One way is to ask Christ to go with you into the past to the time when your wounds were inflicted. Recall for example some occasion when you were bitterly hurt because your offered affection was rejected. Picture the scene, visualise those who were present, recall the words spoken, let yourself feel again the pain of rebuff. Then picture the door opening and Jesus coming in, going up to you, putting his arms round you, telling you to cheer up, that he loves you and will always be with you. Each person must do this as best he can in his own way. But what am I doing in this exercise of imagination? Am I playing a mental game? What I am actually doing is using my imagination in the service of faith. All past times, including my past life, are present to Christ. Further, our past experience lives on, largely unconsciously, and influences us in the present; and so this exercise of faith-imagination is really a means of opening up a shut-away area of our being to the healing river of divine grace. In her paperback, *The Gift of Inner Healing*[7], Ruth Stapleton gives instance after instance where the emotional traumas of childhood have been healed through faith-imagination, enabling a personality whose growth had been stunted to flower into new and vigorous life.

4

Growth in commitment to God proceeds side by side with growth in self-knowledge. The life-enhancing, cleansing Spirit of God, the soul's blood, brings about his work of renewal and restoration largely by arousing and deepening our self-awareness. Whatever enlarges self-knowledge co-operates with the work of the indwelling Spirit. One way in which this precious knowledge can be extended is through the frank acknowledgment of our weaknesses, our hopes and fears, our joys and sorrows and temptations, to a counsellor we can trust. The act of acknowledgment brings in its train a deeper realisation of what we are. It may be that, though it is not necessary matter for the sacrament of absolution, this kind of acknowledgement should sometimes be included with any actual sins in confession. The absolution would then be seen less as the gift of forgiveness and more as the declaration of God's acceptance of us as we are with all our human qualities and idiosyncrasies.

There are many ways of fostering the growth of self-knowledge. Dreams can tell us something about ourselves, especially if we have some knowledge of dream interpretation. They are a language of the unconscious. Part of their function is compensatory, to call the attention of the conscious mind to realities which it is overlooking or neglecting, sometimes in warning, often in encouragement. Dream figures often represent aspects of the dreamer's personality.

[7] Hodder and Stoughton 1977.

Even without much knowledge of dream interpretation a dream by its atmosphere of gaiety or gloom can help the person who reflects upon it to a deeper self-knowledge. But the experiences of waking life can tell us much about ourselves and in a less ambiguous language than that of dreams. Why was I so depressed when my helpful suggestion was ignored? Why am I so absurdly pleased at praise and cast down by blame? Why did I feel pleased at another's discomfiture? Reflection on our over-reactions, on the emotions which surprise us by their strength, can tell us something about ourselves. Again the indignant response of a friend to an innocently intended remark may well tell me something about myself as well as about my friend. There may be something in me visible to my friend but not to me. The abrasive home truth from someone who knows me well may greatly increase my stock of self-knowledge if I am prepared to learn from this disagreeable source.

But there is a psychological fact which when recognised can prove so effective a means of self-knowledge that it deserves to be examined at some length: the fact of projection. Projection, the reading into another of emotions or intentions which are really in ourselves is a universal fact which has been alluded to earlier in this book. It is by no means always a mistake and is one of the ways in which we come to understand our fellows. My own reactions enable me to guess at the reactions of my friend. I get to know what my friend is feeling because I see in him signs of something which I feel in myself. My own inner reactions to the words or the personality of another are a kind of window through which I see him. But just as when you look at the sky through a dirty window you may mistake a smudge on the window for something, a cloud perhaps, in the sky, so you may easily suppose some unknown bit of yourself which he has roused into life to be in him. It is well known that the faults we most dislike in others are faults which our friends sometimes perceive in us, though we may be blind to them ourselves. This fact of projection can help us to discover things in ourselves which we have known and tried to forget or perhaps have never known at all. The persons for whom I have an irrational dislike, those I fear because they embarrass me and make me feel small, those who fill me with distaste or shrinking, may prove my best allies in the search for self-awareness. For they probably in some way represent or symbolise qualities or feelings in myself which are deeply repressed or which I do not wish to own. No doubt my dislikes and fears may have solid grounds in unfriendly behaviour on their part. Even so, their attitude has very likely awakened in me buried emotions, a legacy from my past, which add an irrational strength to my reactions. To take an extreme case a prisoner brought out of solitary confinement for interrogation cannot be expected to have friendly feelings for his interrogator. But in the course of the inquisition he may be seized with a feeling of diabolical hatred against the inquisitor who pesters him with question after question in order to trap him into betraying some secret. Through this experience he could be made aware of an emotion, a potentially destructive force in himself of which previously he had been unaware. To return to more usual experiences a person may irritate me because he caricatures some quality in myself. When I recognise the quality as my own my irritation melts away; I am the problem not he. The vanity which I find unbearable in my acquaintance annoys me because it rouses my own sleeping vanity which I prefer not to know about, for it offends my sense of personal dignity. By facing and owning my suppressed desire to show off I withdraw my projection, I lose my dislike of the acquaintance and I become more human, for I know myself better. I also draw closer to God, who is the God of the real and the true.

A possible method of withdrawing a projection is to picture the person who irritates me as being in myself. The mental picture which I form represents something unknown in me which I seek to know. I shall pray for light to perceive the hidden thing in myself which the picture symbolises. I shall quickly learn to value the picture because it will rid me of my annoyance and bring me peace. The term projection is used by psychology to describe a phenomenon which has been obscurely known since time immemorial. When Jesus warns us against trying to remove the speck from our brother's eye while there is a much larger blockage in our own he shows himself aware of it. Perhaps it was because he observed people's tendency to blame others for faults which were their own that he insists that we must forgive from the heart if we are to be forgiven. We shall be able to do this only if we are able to see the offence of others as a reflection of something which at least in germ is present in us, in other words if we can withdraw our projections. Only by doing so shall we find inward peace. Perhaps this is also part of his reason for telling us to pray for our enemies. When we pray genuinely for those hostile to us or to interests dear to us our feelings towards them change and it becomes increasingly difficult for us to project our own faults on to them. We come to see them as fellow-human beings much like ourselves; we stop hating them.

The fact of projection brings home to us the social nature of mankind. For good and for ill we interpenetrate one another at a level outside our consciousness. It is not fanciful to picture another person as in me; it is the symbolic representation of a fact. The Holy Spirit, the soul's life blood, is the life blood of the human race. In the economy of salvation he draws us into oneness with our fellows. His breath like the wind, reviving and invigorating, circulates to us all. As we make progress in the journey towards the land of wholeness and grow in friendship towards God we shall become increasingly conscious of the interflow between others and ourselves, that in a true sense they dwell in us and we in them. Further, as we journey towards the golden future we continually return to that event in the past which is also a transforming reality in the present, the death on the cross. In the next chapter we shall reflect on one of the ways in which we make contact with and allow ourselves to be changed by the Christ, once crucified but now alive.

10

The Church's Banquet:

THE HOLY EUCHARIST

1

The phrase, the Church's banquet, beckons the imagination in two directions. It speaks of the goal of the human pilgrimage, the land of spices, the joyful feast in God's presence where we shall find the nourishment and fellowship that our souls crave. The food will be the bread of life and the drink the living water of the Spirit who opens our minds to know and our hearts to love. It will be a feast of friendship. We shall see ourselves reflected in the love of friends. We shall see into the hearts of our fellows without any trace of arrogance, we shall be open to them without any sense of shame. In prayer we enter in anticipation the land of wholeness where our humanity will find complete fulfilment. It might be said that to try to describe the life of heaven is to bid our imagination wander in the realm of fantasy. No doubt the promises of God are vastly greater than we can conceive, and it can be taken for certain that the life to come will be full of unforeseeable surprises. But it is better to imagine as best we can than to leave an imaginative blank which will quickly be filled with the guesses of secularised man. We do best, I think, if we picture the celestial feast as the fulfilment of the life of friendship with God already experienced here in its beginnings, a friendship which orients us towards the love of our fellows and the living out of our own truth.

But 'the Church's banquet' speaks not only of the life of heaven but even more of the eucharist, which is both an anticipation of the heavenly life and also the necessary food of the heavenward journey. How can we who live in the twentieth century enter more fully into the meaning of this symbolic rite which presents us with a means

147

of participating in and acting out the story of our redemption? One way might be to suspend disbelief and imagine ourselves to be back in first-century Palestine, to imagine the last supper as though we had been present, to see the events leading up to the crucifixion as though we were contemporary observers, to be with the disciples behind locked doors when Jesus appeared to them alive on Easter Day. Most of us are used to suspending disbelief when we read a novel. We know of course that the world we enter then is the imaginative construction of the author however closely it may be modelled on the real world. But this does not trouble us; and we are willing not only to enter the matter-of-fact world of Barchester under the guidance of Trollope but also the strange and fantastic world of Middle Earth under the spell of Tolkien, with its hobbits and wizards, its elves and dwarfs and ents, with its orcs and goblins. Further, we may learn a great deal about the real world, about human character, even about our own inner motives, by entering into the world of the story and observing how the different people in it think and feel and act. We may end the reading of a great work of literature with a sense of having learnt much of what human life is about. In other words fiction, that is what is feigned or imagined, can be the powerful vehicle of truth.

The eucharistic liturgy has something in common with the story which the great novelist tells. There is an element of story in the eucharist though familiarity may deaden our appreciation of the fact. The eucharist sets out as a great novel the meaning of life and death as this was lived out long ago and so enables us to enter into the meaning and make it our own. Further, just as when reading a novel we enter into another time, the time in which the story is set, so in a sense in the eucharist we pass out of the twentieth century into sacred time, into the central point of salvation history. But of course despite the similarities there are great and essential differences. A great novel does indeed intend to do something to the reader, to enlarge his grasp of the meaning of life and so to change him. The eucharist intends this but a great deal more also. It is designed to enable participants not only to recall a past event but also to encounter a living person. It calls out and expresses their faith in God and strengthens their commitment to his reign. It is meant to change the lives of those who take part in it in the way that a living symbol can change those who open themselves to its power, focusing their imagination, releasing their emotions, mov-

ing them to action. The eucharistic liturgy is an arrangement of
symbols designed to involve the participants deeply in the event of
Calvary and to arouse their capacity to live with something of the
courage and generosity, the faith and love and gentleness of Christ.
A symbol which is alive and powerful is always mysterious; it cannot
be fully grasped. But if it is to have power to bring about radical
change in a person it must be related and in some way belong to
the world in which he lives his life, to his home and family, his work
and leisure and friends, his neighbourhood and his nation. Unless
the symbol can be seen as credible in this everyday context it will
be devitalised and made to seem unreal. Part of the reason for the
weakness of institutional religion today is due to the loss of relevance
of its symbols which appear to have little to do with the contemporary world. They are redolent of an age that is past and no longer
speak with their old power to modern people. Many people are at
work today, theologians, liturgists, pastors, seeking ways of renewing the old symbols or trying to discover new.

The symbolic power of the eucharist is conveyed partly through
its action, what is done, and partly through the accompanying
words whose function is to explicate the meaning of the action. In
the recent revision and updating of the liturgy something is being
done both to make the eucharistic action more significant and to
renew the accompanying language. In the rewriting of the words of
the liturgy there has been an inevitable clash between the need to
retain something of the mystery and poetry that clings to archaic
language, which time and a multitude of associations have hallowed,
and the sharper, more clearly defined meaning which contemporary
language, alas somewhat flat and pedestrian, can give. Liturgists
and pastors together have the task of working out this renewal of
liturgical language. In this chapter I want to reflect on the meaning
of the eucharistic action, especially in relation to the theme of this
book, the growth in a relationship of love and trust towards God
which leads to an outgoing love to our fellows and a living out of
our own humanity.

The eucharist falls into two parts which are normally joined
together but can on occasion be celebrated separately. There is the
liturgy of the word and there is the liturgy of the sacrament, that
is of the eucharist proper. The function of the liturgy of the word
is to prepare the hearts and minds of the people for their proper
sharing in the sacrament which follows it. This chapter will be

concerned with the eucharistic sacrament. Of the liturgy of the word it will be enough to say that it consists principally of prayers, including expressions of penitence and of intercession for mankind, readings from the Scriptures and the preaching of the word. The Scriptures are the record of God's self-disclosure in the history of the Israelite people which came to its climax in the life, death and resurrection of Jesus Christ. The memory of this divine revelation is kept fresh by the readings and its meaning explained and driven home by the sermon. Part of the function of the sermon is to relate the news about God and its expression in the liturgy to the contemporary world, to show how it can be embodied in daily living and to prepare the members of the congregation for the confrontation with Jesus Christ in the liturgy that is to follow and especially when they receive him into their lives in communion.

We referred in the last chapter to the Pauline insight into the meaning of the Christian life as an identification with the dying and rising again of Jesus Christ. The apostle does not mean a literal dying and rising again but rather an attitude of life, clearly exemplified in Christ's life, which death and resurrection aptly symbolise. We explained this as a letting go of the past in order to grasp the present and the future, a letting go of old securities in order to take hold of the new opportunities to which God summons us. In a world at one with God this letting go and taking hold would have been a glorious adventure. In a world estranged from God it has become an adventure from which we shrink in dread. In the passion of Christ we see the agony it caused, the fear, the sweat of blood, and finally the physical torment of a Roman execution. What Jesus endured as he trod the way of the Father's will is not simply an example of heroic endurance and self-sacrifice but a transforming power in those who will open themselves to it. It can liberate us from the fears and the painful memories which hold us in chains and release in us the spirit to face life and the future with something of the courage and generosity of Christ. The eucharist is intended to expose us to the powerful summons of Christ, crucified but alive.

2

One way of understanding the eucharist is as the sharing in a kind of drama. When you watch a serious play at the theatre you get

involved in the tensions and conflicts of the characters as you see
them enacted on the stage and can be deeply moved by them. You
may be made aware of your own feelings, your own problems, of
the meaning of life as you see them enacted before your eyes. The
idea of drama, the representation of truth in action is a clue to the
meaning of the eucharist. Every eucharist is a dramatic representation in which the whole congregation should join of what was
done at the last supper of Jesus with his disciples. But that supper
is significant, like the opening shots of a decisive battle, because of
what followed – the arrest, the trial, the condemnation, the death
by crucifixion and finally the resurrection. By re-enacting the last
supper Christians recall and celebrate all that happened from
Maundy Thursday to Easter Day. In other words, the eucharist,
though in form a meal, is the celebration of a central and decisive
act by which the Creator through Christ is reconciling the world to
himself, ending the estrangement due to sin. This celebratory character of the eucharist makes it not just a meal commemorating
Christ but an act of worship.

At the supper Jesus took bread, gave thanks over it, broke it and
gave to the disciples with the words, 'Take, eat, this is my body.'
These four actions – the taking, the giving thanks, the breaking, the
distributing – have become charged with high significance in Christian thought. I propose now to draw out some of the meaning which
these actions can have for men and women of the twentieth century.

Before the last supper it had been someone's duty to get ready
the bread and wine and the other accompaniments of a passover
meal, if indeed it was a passover meal, which is not certain, for the
evangelists are disagreed on this point. The preparation of the bread
and wine has from very early times been seen as significant. In the
earliest days of the Church it was the custom for members of the
congregation to bring offerings in kind including bread and wine,
some of which was selected for use in the liturgy. Today the getting
ready of the bread and wine has become the task of the clergy and
their helpers. The collection has taken the place of the gifts in kind.
All the same there is an important symbolic meaning in the setting
apart of bread and wine which we cannot afford to lose. In some
churches the sharing of the whole congregation in this action is
expressed through its members being invited to place a wafer of
bread into a ciborium before, or sometimes during the service, for
use in the liturgy. The giving of money in the collection is perhaps

a more realistic as well as a more convenient equivalent today of the ancient bringing of gifts in kind. The people do not come emptyhanded.

The bread and wine set apart for the liturgy stand both for God's bounty in nature and for human life and labour. The bread which sustains us may have been baked from wheat grown in Canada and transported across the Atlantic. It can stand for the whole combined operation of agriculture, industry and commerce without which we should starve. The setting apart of bread stands for the setting apart of our lives supported by food and the labour by which we earn it. Wine stands for the richness and joy of life, our love and friendship, the beauty which delights us, everything which makes life happy. With the exercise of imagination everything that contributes to the setting apart of the bread and wine for the liturgy, from the money put into the collection and the wafer into the ciborium, to the server handing bread and wine, to the celebrant and his taking it and presenting it with prayer, all can be seen to stand for the setting apart of ourselves, our souls and bodies, our work and leisure, our families and our friendships to be consecrated for God's service. If this act is to be more than a formality it must involve some searching of heart and conscience. For we are aligning ourselves with the Lord in his surrendering of himself to the death of the cross. It is not that we are to screw ourselves up to a great act of dedication to the Lord's service. For only God himself can enable us to give ourselves genuinely. Our part is rather to try not to cling to old securities whether personal or material. For whatever we cling to unduly makes us less available to God. One way of loosening our over-attachment to the persons and things we value is to recognise them as God's gifts and to express our gratitude to him for them. Thanksgiving is an effective means of disposing ourselves for God's service.

After Jesus had taken the bread and the cup at the supper he gave thanks. Probably he used the words of the grace familiar to every Jew: 'Blessed are thou, O Lord our God, eternal King, who dost bring forth bread out of the earth'; and over the cup: 'Blessed art thou, O Lord our God, who createst the fruit of the vine.' As the disciples after the resurrection repeated the Lord's action at the supper, the thanksgiving, which followed the presenting of the bread and the cup, came to be seen as the central act of the liturgy and gave it the name eucharist. It is a thanksgiving for 'creation, preservation, and all the blessings of this life', but most of all for the great act of redeeming love by which God in Christ ended in principle the estrangement due to sin. We have just seen thanksgiving as a way of making ourselves available to God. In the thanksgiving prayer of the eucharist our small acts of thanksgiving are incorporated into the great thanksgiving of Christ and his Church. Thanksgiving is the natural and logical way to hallow or consecrate persons or things. Through it we as it were hand things over to their true Owner, gladly acknowledging and assenting to his ownership.

Thanksgiving has a fundamental place in the Christian's pilgrimage to the land of wholeness. Besides being an expression of gratitude it is also the affirmation of faith in the unseen God ceaselessly at work sustaining all things, leading man to his fulfilment and drawing good out of evil. Thanksgiving is a powerful weapon against the mistrust which blocks the channels along which the river of God's grace would flow to heal and liberate. Much that God does in us can be likened to the sowing of seed which can germinate and ripen only if it falls into the soil of faith. Thanksgiving by articulating and expanding faith helps to fertilise the soil in which God's blessings lie. In the eucharistic liturgy we thank God supremely for the Man whose total self-giving to the point of death makes it possible to believe in the love of God, for the Man who came to be our brother, our friend, our food and our life. The thanksgiving opens a door into the past through which the decisive events of Christ's death and resurrection are made present again for us to share in.

There has been fierce controversy in the past about the mode of Christ's presence in the eucharist between men who all believed that he was present in some way. Here I can do no more than set out a personal view. The gospels record the Lord's words, 'Where two or three are gathered together in my name, there am I in the midst of them.'[1] The words do not specifically refer to the eucharist but they clearly apply here; there is a real presence of Christ in the people gathered together in mutual love to celebrate the eucharist. But this, true though it is, is not what most Christians mean by the eucharistic presence, which for them is focused in the consecrated bread and wine. It is round the meaning of the words 'This is my

[1] Matthew 18.20.

body', 'This is my blood', that controversy has circled. We are reflecting on something which we cannot hope fully to comprehend. We must see the words in the context of God's saving purpose for mankind. Many Christians believe that after the prayer of thanksgiving the bread and wine are no longer ordinary bread and wine. A change has taken place but not a physical change. Materially they remain bread and wine, but they are something more, they have taken on a new meaning.

We are here face to face with mystery. Perhaps a trivial instance of change of meaning from the world of everyday life can suggest a way of trying to sound the unfathomable. A piece of paper is of no great value in itself; it is something to write on or light a fire with. But if it is paper of a certain size, shape and texture and has certain marks printed on it it is ten pounds. Materially it is just a piece of paper, but to call it that would be most misleading; it is a ten-pound note. The authority of the Bank of England has made it so and behind the Bank is the State. The authority behind the eucharist is God himself. He who said 'This is my body', 'This is my blood', is the divine Son through whom mankind is being remade. An order to the royal mint will cause any number of bank notes to be printed. Christ had to suffer, die and rise again to fill the bread and wine with their new power and meaning. The bank note is a valuable, though perhaps dispensable, unit in our monetary system. The eucharist is part of the economy of salvation. The eucharistic sacrament is a meal ordained by Christ through which he meets and moulds his disciples down the ages and enables them to identify themselves with him in his dying and rising again. So most Christian believers see in the eucharistic elements the veil which hides the presence of the living Christ, the veil which their faith pierces.

After giving thanks Jesus broke the bread. At first sight this action may not appear to have much significance. But this is not how the first disciples regarded it; and one of the early names of the eucharist was the breaking of bread. From the first it was seen as an action full of meaning. The breaking of the bread had of course the practical purpose of sharing it with those present. The first meaning of the broken and shared bread is the unity of Christians. 'We who are many are one body, for we all partake of the one bread.'[2] One of the early liturgies refers to the many grains of wheat mixed together and baked into a single loaf as a picture of the many Christians knit into one body through Christ. A common allegiance to a leader and a cause can unite men and women of very different temperament and outlook. Christ and the loyalty and trust he evokes is the magnet which draws his disciples into unity. This unity is symbolised by the shared bread. The practice of using small wafers obscures the symbolism of the one loaf and, increasingly, churches are reverting to the primitive practice of breaking a single loaf or piece of bread in the eucharist.

The shared bread of the eucharist speaks of the unity of Christ's followers, but the actual breaking points to another meaning also. For the breaking of the bread taken in conjunction with the words, 'This is my body', reminds us irresistibly of the body broken and bleeding on the cross. The bread was broken to be shared. Christ underwent death in order to share his manhood, his life, with mankind. The gospel records that not long before his death he exclaimed, 'I have a baptism to be baptized with; and how I am constrained until it is accomplished!'[3] He saw his death as a baptism, an immersion in dark waters, and the necessary gateway to the fulfilment of his mission. He felt hampered, his influence narrowed down, by obstacles from which only the passage of death would free him. On another occasion he is recorded as saying 'Unless a grain of wheat falls into the earth and dies, it remains alone; but if it dies, it bears much fruit.'[4] As the loaf had to be broken in order to be shared so Christ had to die to make himself completely available to his disciples.

The shared bread speaks of the unity Christ wills for his disciples, the breaking speaks of the cost of unity. There is a third meaning to which the symbolism points, the breaking of the bread of friendship. If there is to be a truly human unity, the union of friends, there must be an exposing of our hearts, our deepest feelings and beliefs. This we shrink from for it makes us vulnerable to the criticism or ridicule of others. People may take advantage of us if we are too frank about what we really feel. Yet without this openness, deep friendship becomes impossible. The breaking of the bread

[2] 1 Corinthians 10.17.
[3] Luke 12.50.
[4] John 12.24.

speaks not only of Jesus' exposing himself to his friends, one of whom betrayed him. It speaks of the sharing of the bread of friendship. He calls his disciples not servants nor pupils but friends. In the eucharist Christ invites us to his table as his friends. We have drawn near to the very heart of the good news. As we have affirmed more than once before, human misery stems ultimately from a three-fold alienation – alienation from God, alienation from our fellows, alienation from our own true being – of which the alienation from God is the root of the other two. Through Christ, we believe, God has acted to end this alienation by inviting us to be his friends. For only friendship with God, the Power and Wisdom behind and within all things, can give us the inner security which makes it possible both to love our fellows and to live out our own truth. The friendship of the divine-human Son draws us into friendship with the eternal Father.

3

After the breaking of the bread there follows the communion, the distributing of the bread to those present and the sharing of the cup, the eating and the drinking. This is the climax of the eucharist. In the past attention has been fixed perhaps too exclusively on this consummation of the eucharistic drama. We enter more deeply into its meaning if we have opened our minds to the symbolic power of the actions which lead up to it. Communion is a moment of contact, sacramental contact, with the living Christ who has passed through death. We make this contact by faith. When Christ healed the sick and the crippled in Palestine he often used to lay hands on the sick person. This gesture served both to express his purpose to heal and to call out the person's faith. In a similar way Christ touches us in communion, not with this hands but through the sacramental signs of bread and wine. This quasi-physical contact with Christ both calls out our faith and communicates Christ's healing, liberating energy.

St John's gospel records the words of Jesus, 'I am the bread of life,'[5] words which at once call to mind the eucharistic bread. Elsewhere in the gospel eternal life is said to consist in the know-

[5] John 6.35.

ledge of God which Jesus mediates. By this is meant not merely intellectual knowledge but the deep knowledge which only love makes possible, the knowledge of the heart. The feeding on Christ's sacramental body and blood in the eucharist is a means, for some the supreme means, of growing more and more in the transforming knowledge which is eternal life. The change of food and drink into the physical substance of our bodies illustrates a different kind of change, a spiritual transformation and growth as our relationship with God is deepened. But unlike the automatic transformation of food and drink through the natural magic of digestion and metabolism into our flesh and bone, our blood and sinew, the spiritual change cannot come about without our willed co-operation.

The faith by which we co-operate with God's action and gifts is a complex and many-levelled act and attitude. It involves some belief in and understanding of the eucharistic mystery; but it requires even more a willingness to trust in and be committed to Christ and what Christ wills. It must thus enlist areas of our being of which we are not masters. It is the function of what is said and done in the liturgy to focus our imagination on the crucified and risen Christ and so stir our hearts and release our energies in the following of him. We might say that the faith by which we respond to Christ's sacramental encounter with us includes a certain readiness to be changed, a willingness to be led into Christ-like actions, to be drawn towards friendship with our fellows, towards the ending of quarrels and the righting of wrongs. The inner change and growth brought about through Christ's sacramental meeting with us, where this is not resisted but responded to with faith, is the deepening and strengthening of our relationship with God. St John in the prologue to his gospel describes the purpose of Christ's coming in the flesh and blood of a human life as to enable us to become sons of God. God has created us with an affinity for him, with a potentiality for sonship to him. Christ through what he was, did and suffered, enables us to realise this possibility of becoming, despite our human frailty, sons to the Author of our being, sons who are also his friends and fellow workers. Because the eucharist is the food of sonship it is also the food of brotherhood. It is a divinely given means by which men and women are knit into one. Through it the members of the Church of God are bound into a brotherhood of believers.

The drama of the eucharist, the acting out in symbolic rite of the last supper and the passion, death and resurrection of Christ is the normal way in which the community of believers is consecrated, united and empowered for its mission. Through the liturgy celebrated together Christians are renewed to live and act as the Body of Christ, the sign of his presence, the means of his action in the world, and to be servants of the divine rule. Through the eucharist the participants receive a fresh impulse to live as a caring community, fresh vision overcomes discouragement and reawakens hope, new vigour flows into men and women as they go out to their homes and their work to labour for the Kingdom.

As I write these words a feeling of uneasiness comes over me. Is this not an extremely idealistic account of the eucharist and its fruits in people's lives? Does it tally with the character of the actual Christians I know or even with my own experience? This doubt must be faced if the eucharist or indeed Christian life itself is to be understood at all. For if we are honest we are forced to acknowledge an immense gap between the ideal Church, the Church as it is meant to be, the Body of which Christ is the Head and the Holy Spirit, the life-blood, and the often small-minded Christians whom we meet. This contrast between the ideal and the actual is especially marked if we judge by appearances, as to a large extent we must if we judge at all. For it looks as though Christians are largely concerned with raising money to repair church buildings, with maintaining the organisational structure of the Church and, in spiritual and moral questions, with maintaining the *status quo*. But appearances are deceptive. The gap and the contrast have of course existed from the very beginning. St Paul on the one hand addresses Christians as men and women who are 'in Christ' and on the other he warns them against drunkenness, stealing and adultery, to say nothing of the less spectacular sins of arrogance, envy and backbiting. But, 'we are saved by hope';[6] and the circumstances which appear humanly speaking hopeless are the richest soil for the growth of vigorous hope in God.

The more sharply we perceive the contrast between the actual and the ideal, the more we shall be driven to rely on God, the God who brings good out of evil and turns disaster into triumph. What could have seemed more hopeless to the disciples of Jesus on the evening of Good Friday as they reflected on their plight? They had been appointed by Jesus to be his lieutenants in a mission to convert

[6] Romans 8.24 (A.V.).

Israel and mankind; they found themselves a group of men with
shattered illusions and ruined hopes. Yet through the miracle of the
resurrection they were transformed into the leaders of a movement
which swept like a forest fire over the ancient world and is full of
life and vigour today after nineteen centuries. We are saved through
hope. The Christian cannot realise his divine potential by the kind
of automatic process which transforms the chrysalis into a butterfly.
He has to reach out by hope to the freedom and mobility for which
he is destined. To grasp the meaning of the Christian life we have
to let our thought and imagination pass to and fro between the
ideal, the reality of our calling and the goal of our pilgrimage, and
the actual, our feeble and half-hearted response to the Lord's summons, our moral and spiritual infirmity, our distance from our goal.

It is as though we appeal to a boy by addressing him sometimes
as the man he hopes one day to be and sometimes as the irresponsible delinquent he occasionally is. Or, to use a different metaphor,
the mountaineer will sometimes feast his eyes on the mountain peak
he hopes to climb or study photographs of it. But if he seriously
means to ascend the mountain he will have to spend much time in
studying maps and consulting guides. Further, most of the time
during the actual ascent the summit will be out of sight and he will
be concentrating his attention on the small section of the mountain
immediately ahead. Yet as he forces his tired muscles to continue
their effort he will be buoyed up by the hope which the sight of the
mountain top has fired in him. The attention which the Christian
gives to his failures and fallings short must be seen in the context
of the hope that the gospel has set alight in him. It is because he
believes that with God's help he can attain to the land of wholeness,
the place of friendship, the fulfilment of his heart's desire, that he
grieves at his waywardness, his occasional acts of truancy, his bouts
of inertia. And this reflection upon his weakness and his frequent
failures throws him upon the wisdom, power and love of his Creator
and Redeemer.

This chapter's meditation on the meaning of the eucharist has
made no attempt at a complete account. Rather it is a personal
view in which I have especially drawn out its bearing on the healing
of our spiritual ills and our threefold growth in oneness with God,
oneness with our fellows and oneness within our own being. But we
cannot rightly concentrate on our own wholeness without regard to
the wholeness of others; indeed to do this would be self-defeating.

Further, it is in fact impossible to draw a line between those committed to the heavenward pilgrimage and those as yet uncommitted. There are secret and anonymous pilgrims who are deeply committed to the journey and there are professing pilgrims who have not begun to commit themselves. God's love radiates impartially on all mankind and invites all to find in him their fulfilment. I mentioned earlier that in the preparatory part of the liturgy intercessions were offered for all men. But the whole eucharistic liturgy must be understood as intercession as well as thanksgiving. In the naive spirit of liturgical prayer we remind the Father of the death of his beloved Son and beg him for his Son's sake to bless and heal the world of men and women for whom his Son died. But the subject of intercession is so large and important that it must form the principal theme of the next chapter.

11

Engine Against The Almighty:

INTERCESSION

1

At first blush the image of an engine of war, such as might be used by a besieging army to reduce an enemy fortress, is an astonishingly robust metaphor for prayer. Can we suppose that the Almighty will be forced into submitting to our will by the battering ram of our violent and unremitting petitions? The sophisticated modern will dismiss the question as rhetorical, as something beneath his contempt. But the answer which seems so self-evident to us with our over-cerebral attempts to understand the ways of God and man is not in reality at all obvious. For prayer, if it is to express as it should the response of our whole being to God, must give voice to the irrational, the violent, the primitive and the childish in us. The anthropomorphic language which shocks our rational, adult consciousness is the only language which means anything to our irrational depths. The powerful sense of the living God, the Creator of all things and Lord of history, which breathes through the Old Testament, is due in large measure to its unashamed anthropomorphisms. The story of Jacob at the ford of the river Jabbok, wrestling all night with God in the form of a man, and refusing to let his adversary go until he had obtained a blessing, not only strikes the imagination vividly, it also teaches a valuable lesson: there is a prayer which is a wrestling with God.[1] The dialogue between God and Abraham in which the patriarch pleaded that Sodom might be spared from destruction if only enough righteous men could be found there, makes us smile be reminding us irresistibly of two men

[1] Genesis 32.22–31.

bargaining over the price of a camel or a carpet.[2] But it teaches the
lesson that God is open to the persuasion of prayer. The psalms use
vigorous language in their address to God, sometimes appealing to
him to wake up and do something about the plight of his people,
sometimes complaining about his forgetfulness of them.

The New Testament introduces something new into men's
approach to God. The teaching of Jesus about God's fatherly love
for every individual person and the sense of sonship which after
Christ's resurrection was breathed into the disciples by the Holy
Spirit, brought a new intimacy into their prayer to the heavenly
Father. But there is little reduction of the anthropomorphic
language of the Old Testament. In one of his parables Jesus compares God to a lazy judge who is reluctantly induced to try the case
of a poor widow in order to escape from her importunate pestering.[3]
In another he compares him to a man who is unwillingly dragged
out of bed at midnight in order to satisfy a neighbour's request for
bread.[4] Jesus is emphatic in his stress on the need for persistent
prayer: 'Ask, and it will be given you; seek, and you will find, knock
and it will be opened to you.'[5] Equally he insists that our prayer
must be confident. The God we address is a Father infinitely more
ready and able to help than a human father. We ought to count on
his help in the way that a small child takes for granted the help of
a father he knows from experience to be both loving and resourceful.
St Mark records the words: 'Have faith in God. Truly, I say to you,
whoever says to this mountain, "Be taken up and cast into the sea,"
and does not doubt in his heart, but believes that what he says will
come to pass, it will be done for him. Therefore I tell you, whatever
you ask in prayer, believe that you receive it, and you will.'[6] We
know that Jesus loved to startle his hearers with paradoxes which
are not meant to be understood literally but are designed rather to
arrest the imagination and so compel attention to some unknown
or forgotten truth. He sought to shake people out of the rut of their
preconceived notions into a practical recognition of the infinite love
and resourcefulness of the heavenly Father. He must not be inter-
preted by an unimaginative literalism to mean that we can persuade

[2] Genesis 18.22–32.
[3] Luke 18.1–8.
[4] Luke 11.5–8.
[5] Luke 11.9.
[6] Mark 11.23–4.

God to bring about something contrary to his will however much we may be able to believe that he will. All the same he spoke the words deliberately and he meant them to be taken seriously, if not with wooden literalism. At the very least he must have meant that confident prayer opens a way to extraordinary blessings.

In reflecting on the nature of intercession it will be useful to recall the distinction made in an earlier chapter between God's absolute and his permissive will. God's absolute will for all men and women is their salvation, their wholeness, their freedom and fulfilment. On the other hand he is the Author of all that is and permits the evil which flows from the misuse of freedom as well as the good that comes from its right use. Let us look at this by taking the concrete case of human sickness. God permits the operation of the germs and viruses which make us ill. But the evidence of Jesus' ministry of healing strongly suggests that sickness is against God's absolute will, though in sickness as with other ills God is ceaselessly at work bringing good out of evil. There is evidence to suggest that other things being equal a strong faith in God reduces a person's liability to falling ill and makes his recovery swifter. Perhaps Jesus is telling us that many of the evils which God permits would be swept away if we had enough faith. Personally I think that Jesus challenges us to use our imagination to picture the thing we desire as already granted by God. For imagination can awaken hope and diminish the inner mistrust which saps our confidence. The blessings which God will give in response to faith are more and better than we can imagine. What we picture in our minds and confidently pray for is a kind of symbol of the things beyond our imagining that God intends for us; and what we actually receive may be other than what we had hoped for. Jesus prayed that his cup of agony might be taken away; the answer he received was the strength to drink it.

2

Many of those engaged in the ministry of healing seem to imply that the reason why those who having been prayed for remain unhealed is due either to lack of faith or lack of perseverance in praying. The lack of faith and perseverance may not necessarily be that of the sick individual but also that of those ministering to him and praying for him, indeed to the small faith of the Christian community of which he is a member. Let us take as an example of this confident faith the teaching of Jim Glennon, Canon of the Anglican Cathedral of Sydney, Australia. He takes the words of Jesus quoted above, 'Whatever you ask in prayer believe that you receive it and you will,' quite literally. There is a proviso which he insists on; you must first commit yourself to Christ and inwardly resolve to follow him; faith is not a matter of mental gymnastics but involves life commitment. But granted this real commitment to Christ you are to pray confidently and having done this you are to thank God for granting your prayer. Even though after praying for the recovery of your health you are conscious of no change whatever in your condition you are to thank God for granting your petition and go on thanking him until your recovery is complete. It is as though a seed of healing has been planted in response to believing prayer but needs time to grow in view of obstacles to health that are hindering it. Canon Glennon gives a number of instances of this believing prayer being rewarded with the recovery of health. Perhaps the most remarkable of his instances is that of a twelve-year-old hunchback boy declared incurable by the doctors. His parents prayed the prayer of faith and thanked God daily for healing their son. For some while they could detect no sign of improvement but they continued day after day with their thanksgiving. After a time they thought they noticed a slight change for the better and bit by bit as they continued their thanksgiving they noted further improvements as the pressures upon the vertebrae which were causing the humpback condition gradually eased and the back began to straighten. At the end of three years the boy's back was straight and he was able to take strenuous exercise and live a normal life. This is one exceptionally striking instance out of hundreds which those engaged in the ministry of healing have described. It is seldom possible to provide proof that prayer was the decisive factor in any particular instance of healing, even when the person healed and his closest friends are convinced that it was. But the cumulative persuasiveness of instance piled on instance is overwhelming. There are however very many who have sought healing by believing prayer and have not found it. To examine the possible reasons for the apparent failure of prayer for healing will, I think, shed light on the nature of intercession in general and not merely on prayer for the sick.

Father Francis Macnutt, the Dominican friar, in his book, *Heal-*

ing, looks at eleven reasons why healing does not take place when prayed for, of which I shall consider a few. The first reason he gives is lack of sufficient faith. It would seem that a person's faith must have grown to a certain intensity before he can become a channel of God's healing. The scepticism about God, which is part of the secularised atmosphere we breathe in, subtly weakens our faith. As we have seen, a living faith is much more than bare belief but includes commitment to God and trust in him; and this solid sub-structure of faith can grow stronger indefinitely. Perseverance in prayer with thanksgiving as described above is clearly a method of toughening faith.

One of the obstacles to being healed is sin, by which is meant not the falling short which is common to everyone but the clinging to resentment, the refusal to forgive and other similar attitudes which a person is unwilling or unable to give up. Such attitudes estrange a person from the source of healing and block the flow of the life-giving waters. Father Macnutt describes an occasion when a group had prayed for a sick sister without any apparent effect. When it was suggested to the sister that she might be harbouring resentment she admitted that this was so and she begged forgiveness. Immediately after that her healing began to take place. It seems possible that this is the explanation of the way Jesus acted in the story of the paralysed man brought to him on a stretcher as recorded in St Mark's gospel, Chapter two. Jesus's first words to the man were, 'My son, your sins are forgiven.'[7] Perhaps he perceived that the man's burdened conscience was a barrier to his healing and only when his mind was at rest did Jesus tell him to get up and walk.

It seems that it is important to pray for specific benefits and not for a general blessing when we seek healing, and perhaps in other contexts too. It is partly that to ask for the specific demands more faith than to ask for a general improvement. When the blind beggar, Bartimaeus, was brought to Jesus it was obvious what was the matter with him. But Jesus asked him, 'What do you want me to do for you?'[8] He wants the man to put his need into words and so make his faith more specific. It takes courage to ask publicly and with confidence for the healing of blindness. But it is important to

[7] Mark 2.5.
[8] Mark 10.46.

be specific for another reason, especially when seeking the healing of the emotional wounds of the past referred to in an earlier chapter. It seems that often each painful memory has to be brought to light and healed. Sometimes after prayer symptoms are removed or at least reduced; but if the underlying trouble has not been uncovered and dealt with, the improvement will not be maintained and the symptoms will return. It is not only in the sphere of physical health that we can be over-concerned with symptoms to the neglect of the underlying cause. We often seek to be rid of temptations which are in fact symptoms of some deep-down malaise, the tell-tale column of smoke which discloses the presence of fire smouldering out of sight. The temptations are of value as pointers to a hidden disorder which otherwise would have been overlooked.

Another reason why prayer for healing is not granted is what might be called presumption, which is of various kinds. There is the presumption which looks on prayer as an alternative to the doctor and refuses medical help. There is the ignoring of elementary rules of health and hygiene and expecting prayer to make good their neglect. Some people drive themselves to the point of physical or nervous breakdown and expect prayer to enable them to continue to over-drive themselves. There is a wisdom of the body or the seed of it in every man through which God himself guides those who rely on it. The presumptuous ignore the voice of this inner wisdom or perhaps have never learnt to listen to it.

Another reason why prayer for healing is seemingly unanswered is that the sick person is sometimes unconsciously attached to his illness and does not want to get well. Emily Neal in her book, *The Healing Power of Christ*, describes the case of a somewhat possessive woman in middle life who, on going to live with her married daughter, fell seriously ill and required much attention from her daughter and son-in-law. She sought and prayed for healing, but unconsciously she was enjoying the attention that her illness won for her and was content with her condition. Despite both prayer and medical help her health failed to improve. Eventually she was brought to recognise that she loved the power to dominate the household which her illness gave her. The realisation of her selfishness led her to a change of heart followed by a swift recovery from her illness.

Much illness is caused by social conditions which provoke anger, resentment and a sense of frustration. This may be found at its most acute in the home. It is a common occurrence for men and women who have entered hospital for treatment, to recover in the caring environment which they find there, to return home cured and promptly fall ill again. The pressures of his social environment may be the reason why a person who has prayed for healing remains unhealed. In such a case the right object of prayer perhaps should be the healing of the antagonisms and distrust in the home and the removal of the obstacles to harmony there. This opens up the large subject of the Christian attitude to the ills of society and how far these should have a place in his concerns and his prayers.

People have different gifts and different vocations. Some are called to enter politics, whether national or local, and to serve their fellow-men in this way. But everyone has a duty as a citizen to promote the well-being of his neighbourhood and his nation. Whatever we are rightly concerned about should have a place in our prayers. I believe that in praying here it is important, as in prayer for the sick, to be specific and detailed. The reason for this is not at all to give directions to infinite Wisdom how he can best influence the course of events. We bring to God our concern for particular objects rather than the general betterment of things because the concrete calls out a more vigorous act of faith. Further, a definite object provides a focus which can help to prevent us from being carried away by unreal hopes and fears. For this reason too I believe it is better to pray about what we know of directly rather what we know only at second hand. It is better to pray for people than for causes or parties. I may not know anything about the prime minister except at second hand through the media; but I know him or her to be human and so subject to similar temptations to my own; and I know too that he or she is in a better position than most to further the common good.

Returning to the subject of prayer for the sick and the reasons why sometimes such prayers are seemingly unanswered, there is one final reason that needs to be looked at. Can there be a redemptive power in sickness? Is a person sometimes left unhealed in order that through his weakness and suffering he can be a channel of divine help to others? St Paul regarded the persecution and the hardship which he underwent in the course of his missionary journeys as a sharing in the sufferings of Christ. Can sickness ever be regarded in this way? It is possible that what St Paul calls his 'thorn in the flesh', 'a messenger of Satan to harass me'[9] was an illness. It is clear that weakness and pain can sometimes elicit from a person a stronger trust in and commitment to God. Emily Neal describes an occasion when she ministered in a healing service while a damaged spine was causing her such acute pain that doctors tried to restrain her from taking part in the service. Exceptional blessings occurred as a result of her ministry on this occasion and she felt herself in an unusual degree the channel of Christ's healing power. It is part of long-established tradition that we can sometimes suffer vicariously, that in order to help others we have to enter into their condition by empathy and sometimes this empathy is extended into an actual enduring of pain on behalf of the other. Those who engage in a ministry of prayer for others must expect sometimes to bear the burdens of those for whom they pray.

There is an extensive literature concerned with the ministry of healing through prayer and other spiritual means, from which I have quoted from three authors,[10] all of them engaged in this ministry. Some of those ministering in this way affirm confidently that all sickness would be healed given sufficient faith. What is to be said to this claim? I state my own opinion that those who speak thus are yielding to the preacher's temptation to over-simplify a mystery which is more complex than they allow in order to drive home an important point. But the perhaps legitimate exaggerations and simplifications of rhetoric must not be erected into an absolute principle. Sickness is an evil which is contrary to the absolute will of God. We can therefore pray with confidence for the healing of the sick. I believe that a great deal of sickness will yield to confident and persevering prayer. I believe too that God will invariably grant to this prayer, if not always the recovery of physical health, at any rate some spiritual blessing, such as an increased faith or love or patience. But I do not believe that in the complexities of a world estranged from God we can assume that it is always God's will to cure a person's sickness. Arrogance, cruelty, hatred, greed and the selfish exploitation of man by man are, I believe, much greater evils than sickness. And so long as the greater evil remains I do not think we can expect to banish the lesser. Further, though I have great

[9] 2 Corinthians 12.7.

[10] The books referred to are *Your Healing is Within You* by Jim Glennon, Hodder and Stoughton 1978. *Healing* by Francis Macnutt, Ave Maria Press 1974. *The Healing Power of Christ*, Emily Neal, Hodder and Stoughton 1978.

sympathy for the growth of healing through spiritual means as part of the Christian Church's mission to the whole person, body as well as soul, I think it is easy to become so concerned about the healing of the sick as to lose a sense of proportion.

3

I have considered at some length intercession in relation to the sick, partly because sickness is a trouble which directly or indirectly affects everyone, partly because the practice of praying for the recovery of the sick is universal among Christians. Further many lessons based on empirical evidence can be learnt from the experience of those engaged in a healing ministry relying on intercession, which are applicable to all kinds of intercession. I would single out in particular the importance of praying with the confidence which expects an answer, of persevering and not giving up too soon, and of being specific, praying about definite, concrete objects rather than generalities. People hesitate sometimes to pray for the spiritual or moral good of others for fear of being guilty of self-righteousness, of concerning themselves with the speck in their brother's eye and forgetting the plank in their own. This difficulty can be overcome by praying in the plural and including ourselves in our prayer for others. It is certainly of greater importance to pray for liberation from the tyranny of spiritual arrogance or the habit of running down all and sundry than for the cure of arthritis or pneumonia. It is probably better to pray for good than against evil, for the healing of relationships and the strengthening of love than against recrimination and anger, for a growing concern for truth-speaking than against lying and evasion.

It looks as though there were two phases in the ministry of Jesus. In the first phase he travelled Palestine, proclaiming the imminent reign of God, summoning men to change their lives and commit themselves to God and the new order which God was about to establish. In proof of his authority and the authenticity of his message he healed large numbers of sick people and liberated many who were demon-possessed. Crowds flocked to him and he gathered a body of disciples. The first phase looked like triumphant success. But his success roused the opposition of the religious authorities, shocked at the novelty of his teaching and at the authority with which he spoke and alarmed at his growing influence. The second phase looks towards the deliberate challenge to the authorities in Jerusalem and its sequel, the death on the cross. In the first phase it seemed that he was battling especially with the lesser evil of sickness, in the second with the greater evil of sin, the fundamental estrangement from God of which sickness is one of the consequences, a task immeasurably more difficult. He healed sickness and cast out demons with a word of command, but the conflict with the powers of darkness meant agony of soul and body and death on the cross.

To speak of two phases as though there was a clearly marked division between them is to over-simplify; a foretaste of the cross was present from the beginning, nor did Jesus cease to heal the sick when he set his face towards Jerusalem. But the two stages in the ministry of Jesus point to two emphases in the lives of his followers. Everything that affects the physical and mental well-being of men and women on this earth is the right and proper concern of Christians. This concern will be not only for the healing of the sick but for the elimination or reduction of the conditions that foster ill-health: extreme poverty, bad and insufficient housing, insanitary conditions etc. The modern welfare state has done much to get rid of extreme poverty and to raise the standard of living of the poor. But the material blessings which the state provides have brought into clearer light the limitations of what state action can do for human well-being. There is a danger that the tendency to look upon the state as the universal provider will both weaken the sense of divine providence and undermine individual initiative. It is not so easy however to push God out of human life as is sometimes supposed. There have always been a few people, especially among the comfortably off, who have known that men cannot live by bread alone. The enormous increase in the world's wealth, which modern science and technology have brought about, has disseminated this knowledge far and wide in every class of society. A growing disillusionment with a society which gives an exaggerated importance to material and this-world values has made many people aware of a previously unsuspected spiritual hunger. This is at bottom, I believe, the desire for God though it is not usually understood in such simple terms. Despite a turning away from the Church as an institution which appears both wedded to the past and bound up with the material values of which they are suspicious, many people today are showing signs, both positive and negative of this spiritual hunger. Among the positive signs are the growing interest in oriental religion, in schools of meditation, largely but not wholly of oriental inspiration, and in books on mysticism and prayer. Among the negative signs the chief are those which indicate disillusionment with the established order and a weakening of loyalty to it: on the one hand there is the increase of drug abuse, the growth of alcoholism, the excessive stimulation of sex and the increasing use of other escape routes into fantasy; on the other there is the growing resort to violence. If there is any truth in this description of the contemporary situation it follows that our intercession for the sick should include those who are spiritually hungry, those who have lost their way, those who are suffering from the boredom and aimlessness prevalent today.

4

Genuine intercession is costly and makes heavy demands on both time and spiritual energy. Not words but a heart and soul committed to God make intercession powerful. There are two basic movements in intercession. First there is the opening of our hearts to those for whom we pray, using our imagination to picture their plight, empathising with them. Then, second, it means the opening of ourselves to God on their behalf. A vivid picture of the practice of intercession is given in *The Undistorted Image*[11] in which Father Sofrony sketches the life of the Russian staretz, Silouan. When a young monk, Silouan, was put in charge of one of the numerous workshops of his monastery on Mount Athos, where migrant workers from pre-revolutionary Russia, usually young men, worked for a pittance in order to take something home to their wives and families in their native land, it soon became known that, unlike those in the other workshops, the workmen under Silouan's supervision worked hard and contentedly and were completely honest. When asked about his method of supervision he explained that all he did was to assign each man his task at the beginning of the day and to promise to pray for him while he worked. He then went to his cell and prayed for each of them in turn, remembering them with love and compassion. Presently his heart would become

[11] Faith Press 1958.

absorbed in God and he would forget them. Later they would return to his mind, this time enfolded in the love of God. We see in the intercession of this saintly monk the double movement of compassionate love for his fellows and of deep commitment to God. We see this double movement in the prayer of Jesus in John chapter seventeen. 'For their sake I consecrate myself.'[12] This prayer of Jesus is not for the world, not for people in general, but for those whom the Father had given him, the tiny group of the disciples in the first place and then for those who would come to believe through their words. He prays that they may be sanctified, that is that they may be God-protected and God-centred, and that they may be made one. The unity prayed for by Christ is a spiritual unity like the unity of the Godhead, a unity of mutual love. The prayer of Jesus given by St John expresses an intention, a current of purpose and desire, which flows through his whole life and flows most strongly in the concluding hours of his passion and death. Here we see intercession translated into action and suffering. It is the consecration, the offering up, of his whole being to God on behalf of his disciples.

It is in the light of Christ's passion and death that we must understand the words recorded in St John: 'Whatsoever ye shall ask the Father in my name, he will give it you.'[13] To pray in the name of Christ must mean something more than a verbal reference to Christ at the end of a prayer. It must mean an identification with Christ's aims, with the things that matter to him, with his whole attitude, not only in our praying but in our whole life. It should not make our prayer less confident but it should make us realise the price we may be required to pay. Those who are led to identify themselves with Christ in his self-consecration on behalf of mankind will have to undergo, in some form or other, something of the weakness and defencelessness of Christ. But no one can pray this prayer of self-consecration genuinely except under the impulse of the Spirit. 'We do not know how to pray as we ought, but the Spirit himself intercedes for us with sighs too deep for words.'[14] All true prayer is Spirit-inspired whether or not it is realised to be so; as a

[12] John 17.19.
[13] John 16.23 (A.V.).
[14] Romans 8.26.

person grows in spiritual perceptiveness he becomes increasingly conscious of his dependence on the Spirit.

At all stages of the spiritual life prayer for others is important, though the manner of interceding will change as commitment to God and our fellows grows. Also differences of temperament and make-up will be reflected in differing methods used in interceding. Some for example will pray by a simple naming of a person in the presence of God, others by ejaculatory prayer, yet others by saying the Our Father with some particular person or group in mind. Some are drawn to the use of lists of those to be prayed for, others are repelled by them. For myself, though lists are not congenial, I cannot do without a reminder of the names of people I know and might otherwise forget. Recalling their names helps to stretch and widen the concern for others with which I try to approach God.

The subjective effect of intercession is important especially in the early stages of spiritual growth. I think that one reason why Jesus tells us to pray for our enemies is that this act of generosity towards them will help to overcome our incipient hatred. Some of those who have undergone harsh treatment in prison or concentration camps have found that by praying for their prison guards and interrogators they were freed from all feelings of enmity and were able to feel warmth and sympathy for them as fellow-human beings. What is true of the extreme situation of a political prisoner trying to love his accusers and gaolers is true of us who, in the unheroic conditions of daily life, try to love those whose personality grates on us or who oppose our aims and despise our values. No doubt a person who believes in intercession at all will pray for those who are dear to him. It is doubly important to pray for our *bête noir*, at least if it is someone we see much of. For this is the surest way of ridding ourselves of the poison of an antipathy, perhaps mingled with contempt, which if it is acquiesced in must cloud our relationship with God.

Intercession if it is genuine is a powerful restorative of relationships under threat. It is necessary to qualify this affirmation with the word genuine, for much that passes for intercession is a kind of make-believe, a going through the motions of praying, with the heart not involved at all. The person who gets on my nerves, justifiably or not, takes on in my mind qualities which may be more in myself than in him. I tend to see him not as a person in the round but in the distorting mirror of my prejudice and dislike. The qualities that annoy me in him are enlarged and exaggerated, so that the picture I form of him in my mind is a bad caricature of the person as he truly is. Unfortunately I am apt to take the caricature for the real person and pray for the caricature if I pray at all. This is not genuine praying. Because of this tendency to stereotype people and diminish them in our minds I believe it is important to follow the counsel of St Paul and join petition with thanksgiving. To thank God for a person I dislike wakes me out of an unhappy fantasy. It helps me to see the person as someone created by God with many good qualities which I cannot in justice deny. I can begin to see him from his own point of view, as a person with worries and burdens like my own, possibly finding it as difficult to get on with me as I with him. After a course of thanksgiving for my bugbear I find my attitude to him has changed and I can pray for him genuinely, wishing him well from the heart. The linking of petition with thanksgiving and praise illustrates the double movement in intercession, towards God in commitment to him and his Kingdom and towards our fellows in love and compassion. The love of God and neighbour mutually strengthen each other. Intercession is one of the ways in which we bring home to ourselves our membership in one another. For as John Donne affirms: 'No man is an island, entire of itself; every man is a piece of the continent, a part of the main.'[15]

[15] *Devotions XVII.*

12

Something Understood:

THE GROWTH OF WISDOM

The final phrase of George Herbert's poem brings us down from the heavenly regions where lives the paradise bird with gorgeous plumage and nightingale song, down from the milky way, the vastnesses of outer space, which like the bells of Bemerton Church or Salisbury Cathedral summon us to worship the Creator, to alight gently upon the homely acres of familiar earth. Prayer is something understood, it enriches the mind, it makes us wise. The words awaken echoes from some verses of Psalm 73, which would have been familiar to Herbert in the Coverdale version of the Book of Common Prayer. 'Then thought I to understand this, but it was too hard for me, until I went into the sanctuary of God. Then understood I the end of these men.'[1] The sanctuary, the meeting place with God, is the place of understanding. The modern reader is uncomfortable about some of the Psalmist's reasoning. We understand readily enough his preoccupation with the problem of evil, but we do not all like his way of stating it. He seems to worry too much about the prosperity of the wicked and we are shocked at his solution of the problem. 'Then understood I the end of these men; how thou dost set them in slippery places and castest them down and destroyest them.'[2] We are inclined to judge him unfairly by the standards of our day which are humane in theory however inhuman in practice. But he gives us the precious reminder that wisdom is born in the sanctuary of God and later he movingly confesses his blindness and lack of insight: 'So foolish was I and ignorant, even

[1] Psalm 73.15–16 (Coverdale).
[2] Ibid. vv. 16–17.

as it were a beast before thee. Nevertheless I am alway by thee, for thou holdest me by thy right hand.'[3]

I have described the Christian journey as a growth into an ever-closer friendship with God which expresses itself in an outgoing love for our fellows and an inner peace which is the fruit of a growing order and harmony within ourselves. Out of this intimacy with God wisdom is born. This is a gift greater than cleverness, than mental agility. It is something more than a penetrating intellectual grasp of facts and truths. It is a vision of men and women and things, of life and death, possible only to those far gone in friendship with God. Long intimacy with God has set such people free from personal and parochial prejudices and enables them to view the world with something of the largeness of the divine compassion. Tolerance is too negative a word to describe the generous appreciation of those who have grown wise in the sanctuary of God for persons, opinions and attitudes differing from and perhaps antagonistic to their own. Prayer has taught them to rejoice in the manifold variety of creation and delivered them from all desire to condemn their fellows.

The indwelling of God in the soul's centre is one of the recurring themes of this book. The Christian journey, the pilgrimage of the heart, can be understood as a process of centring, a learning to find the way with increasing certainty to this inner sanctuary. The stages of the journey are the different phases of this movement towards the centre, of the effort to respond more and more sensitively to the divine authority within. There is the initial battle with the tendencies, the habits, the interests which are opposed to the Godward search. There is a later stage when we begin to be lit by rays of light from the centre, which in our estranged condition seem like rays of darkness but which nevertheless draw us like a magnet despite our incomprehension. There is the stage further on still when friendship with God begins to be felt as life's supreme treasure and increasingly everything is judged in the light and warmth of this friendship. This indwelling of God within the soul is not explicitly referred to in Herbert's sonnet, except for the line, 'God's breath in man returning to his birth'. The immense range of metaphors suggests rather the soul's dwelling in God. Prayer is the soul in paraphrase. To paraphrase a sentence is to enlarge upon and

[3] Ibid. vv. 21–22.

draw out its meaning. Prayer expands the soul and enables it to
tread the milky way and visit the land of spices. But we must not
be literalist in interpreting spatial metaphors. The metaphor of the
divine presence in the soul's centre illuminates and makes vivid the
reality of God's ever-present action within us, which Herbert's
kaleidoscope of images suggests in other ways.

We have by no means exhausted the images of our poem. For
example there is the phrase, 'reversèd thunder', which is perhaps
an expression of the prayer of protest. Thunder has from time
immemorial been thought of as a sign of God's anger. 'Reversèd
thunder' would seem to mean man's wrath against God. 'The kingdom of heaven has suffered violence, and men of violence take it by
force,'[4] said Jesus enigmatically. Prayer ought to be the honest
expression of our feelings and to ask questions about and to protest
against the world's injustice can be a much more valid prayer than
to express our limp acquiescence in things as they are. Again, 'a
kind of tune which all things hear and fear' can set the imagination
alight. The voice of prayer is powerful, it influences the hearts of
men and the course of events. Unlike the Siren's song whose loveliness enticed sailors to shipwreck, it is a song which summons men
to new and abounding life. But it is a tune that men fear because
the new life of which it sings can be grasped only by letting go of
old and familiar habits, a letting go which feels like death. Yet we
cannot rid our minds of its dangerous haunting melody which
summons us to take leave of old security and set out across unknown
seas.

The theme of God's indwelling in the soul's centre which has run
through this book could be expressed in another way by saying that
God who is present throughout the universe as a sustaining Cause
and an inexhaustible and unsleeping Influence is most accessible to
man within his own being. A second and equally recurrent theme
is the self-disclosure of the transcendent God in Jesus Christ and
especially in the weakness and nakedness of the cross. It is this
revelation of the vulnerability of God that enables the Christian to
hold on to his conviction of God's utter trustworthiness without
shutting his eyes to life's tragic dimension. For if the gospel is to be
indeed good news it must come as a message of healing and deliverance to man in his lostness, his compulsive hatred of and cruelty

[4] Matthew 11.12.

to himself and his fellows, his loneliness, his depression, his frustration, and all the many forms which human misery can take. It is
because God has identified himself with man by undergoing something like the worst that could happen that he is able to persuade
those who have strayed furthest from their true goal of the possibility
of redemption and so awaken hope. Only those who have plumbed
profoundly the depths of man's threefold estrangement are able
fully to grasp the hope of life beyond life which Christ's resurrection
promises.

This book has been a personal one in the sense that I have made
no attempt to give a complete account of the Christian life, even in
a compressed form, and have concentrated on those points which
seemed to me of outstanding importance. This means that I have
left on one side matters which another might well feel ought to have
been included. Some will feel that something should have been said
about the nature of the authority which Christians accord to the
Bible, from which I have quoted extensively. Others will feel that
I should have been more precise in what I have said about the
authority and the boundaries of the Church. But each of these
subjects is both complex and controversial, and to have dealt with
them adequately would have interfered with the purpose of the book
and destroyed its balance. Though I write as an Anglican the book
has in mind all who profess and call themselves Christians. As the
perceptive reader will have recognised I am greatly indebted to the
spiritual tradition of the Catholic Church of the West. I have learnt
much too from Protestant Evangelical spirituality especially where
this has been enlivened by the charismatic revival. I have also
learnt something from the wisdom of the East and more from the
secular pyschology of the West.

Though I have described the pilgrimage of the heart as Christians
understand it I am well aware that the pilgrimage is everyman's
journey whether he be Christian or not. For God is, I believe,
working for the salvation, the total healing and liberation of all
men. I have written for Christians because Christianity is the only
religion I know from within, not out of any disrespect for other
religions or their adherents. Further, as this book will have made
evident, I believe that the concrete and particular must be given
priority over sweeping generalities. It would be ridiculous for me to
give advice to Hindus or Buddhists, to Muslims or Jews, as to how
they should pursue the human journey. If any of them should

chance to read this book, as I hope some will, I believe they will be more helped by my description of the spiritual journey as a Christian sees it than if I had tried to tailor the description to their supposed requirements. For I believe that God not only invites all men to find their wholeness and freedom in a relationship with himself, but that he also guides them from the place where they are. The starting point for each person will be what, through his response to the religious and cultural influences which have moulded him, he has become. I believe God leads the vast majority of Hindus by a Hindu path and of Muslims by a Muslim one. I do not believe that all religions are equally true or helpful to their adherents, any more than I believe that all cultures are equally rich or that all men are equally wise. Nor do I rule out God's drawing a person to transfer his allegiance from one faith to another. Indeed in the ecumenical climate of today and the growing respect and friendliness between the adherents of different religions this is likely to happen more frequently in the future than in the past. But these will be the exceptions; and I believe that God draws the great majority of men and women to find their way to him within the religion in which they have grown up.

Am I being disloyal to my Christian allegiance in thinking that the other great religions can be a way of salvation for their adherents? There are many Christians who will say that I am. They will say that there can be no salvation except through the conscious acceptance in this life of Jesus Christ as Lord and Saviour. And they will quote such texts as 'There is salvation in no one else, for there is no other name under heaven given among men by which we must be saved.'[5] Nevertheless, despite the disagreement of some Christians, I do not believe my position to be in any way inconsistent with my belief in the Incarnation. For I believe with the author of the fourth gospel that the Word who was made flesh in the manhood of Jesus Christ is the Light of all men everywhere and at all times. I believe him therefore to be the light not only of Christians but of Hindus and Buddhists, of Muslims and in an especial way of Jews. Whatever is true in those religions, so I believe, comes from the Word, however their adherents may understand it. I must add that owing to the estrangement known as original sin, referred to a number of times in this book, all human

[5] Acts 4.12.

understanding of the things of God is not only limited but confused and intermingled with error. Further, our understanding is always largely influenced, though not wholly determined, by our culture. As a Christian I do not except myself nor other Christians wiser than myself from these limitations. My belief is that Jesus Christ is altogether unique, not only among men but among religious prophets and founders. My hope is that in the distant future the day will come when the adherents of other religions, without sur-rendering their own peculiar strengths and insights, will acclaim Jesus Christ as the Crown and Fulfilment of their own faith. This does not mean that I think that Christians have everything to give to those of other faiths and nothing to receive. On the contrary, I believe that there is need of a two-way traffic especially in spirit-uality and the different ways of expressing the truth of our humanity.

The Godward journey is a journey on which every individual is launched, all unknowingly, at birth. It is possible, alas, so I believe, to exclude ourselves from the destination we were meant to reach. For God will not, perhaps cannot, force persons to embrace salva-tion against their wills and against the whole set of their characters. But it may not be so easy as has sometimes been assumed to reject or miss the wholeness and freedom we are destined for, despite all appearances to the contrary. The fact that some men doubt and others deny the existence of God does not place them outside the range of God's caring providence. No one can silence God's voice as it calls him to search for truth, to rejoice in beauty, to choose good and refuse evil. Just as many, I believe, will be surprised to discover that there is a life after this life, so I also believe that many a professed atheist will be astonished to find out that God is not the tyrant, the ogre of his imagining, that he had refused to believe in, but is in truth the object of his secret longing, of his heart's desire. In the words of the Catholic poet, Francis Thompson, 'Some may perchance with vague surprise have stumbled into Paradise.'[6] The grounds for this ultimate optimism is the character of the Author of the human story, as disclosed uniquely nineteen hundred years ago in Jesus Christ, his life, his teaching, his death on the cross and his resurrection. In the words already quoted of the thirteenth-century Englishwoman, theologian and mystic, Julian of Norwich,

[6] 'Epilogue' to *A Judgement in Heaven*, Francis Thompson, O.U.P. 1946.

'All shall be well and all shall be well and all manner of things shall be well.'[7] For, to quote St Irenaeus, Bishop of Lyons at the end of the second century, 'the glory of God is man fully alive.'[8] Man is at present only half alive, he is imperfectly human, he is as yet in the making. God destines him to become human through and through, to become fully and abundantly alive in the land where in the company of his fellows he will explore without end the unfathomable mystery of the Godhead.

---

[7] *Revelations of Divine Love*, Chapter 32.
[8] *Against Heresies* iv.20.7.

Appendix:

PRAYER AND DIFFERENT TYPES
OF PEOPLE

In trying to suggest how different types of people may best pray I shall take as my starting point Carl Jung's[1] descriptive analysis of human nature. It is easy to criticise this analysis as too neat and contrived. No two men or women have identical characteristics and it is impossible to fit human beings into any scheme without leaving out many individual qualities. Jung himself acknowledged every human being to be a profound mystery. But just because people are so various Jung's system, despite its inevitable omissions and simplifications, does help to bring some order out of the chaos of human differences. There are other theories of human types of which that of William Sheldon, based on physical constitution is probably the best known.[2] According to this theory every man and woman can be understood as a mixture in different proportions of three physical components which Sheldon terms endomorphy, ectomorphy, mesomorphy. The endomorphic constitution is that of the short, jolly friendly individual inclining to fatness; the mesomorphic is the strong, athletic person, competitive and aggressive; the ectomorphic is thin, unathletic, sensitive, imaginative, intellectual. These types being closely linked to bodily constitution have the advantage of being fairly easy to recognise. I have preferred Jung's typology because it helps far more than does Sheldon's to explain the inner dynamics of men and women. The fact that it is not easy to be sure

[1] For Jung's theory of types see *Psychological Types*, Volume VI, of his collected works, Routledge and Kegan Paul 1971. There is a brief summary of his theory in his *Modern Man in Search of a Soul*, Chapter four, Routledge 1933.
[2] There is a summary of Sheldon's theory in Chapter eight of *The Perennial Philosophy* by Aldous Huxley, Fontana 1958.

to which Jungian type another person or even you yourself belong is by no means altogether a disadvantage. For every man and woman is fundamentally mysterious; and uncertainty as to a person's type hinders the over-confident assessment which is an insuperable obstacle to any deep understanding.

Attitude Types: Introvert and Extravert

For Jung the most fundamental division of types is that between what he calls the introvert and the extravert. The extravert turns with a ready welcome to the world outside him, the introvert to the world within. If I am an extravert the people, the things, the happenings around me will be of supreme importance. It will be essential to my peace of mind to be on good terms with these. If I am an introvert I shall tend to be on the defensive against the world outside me. What will matter most is that I be true to my own self, to my own ideas and feelings, to my own vision. At all costs I must preserve my inner integrity. It is a mistake to suppose that one type is superior to another except in particular circumstances or in the carrying out of particular tasks. Each type has its strong and weak points and each tends to underrate the other. The introvert tends to regard the extravert as superficial, the extravert to write off the introvert as unpractical. The types in fact complement each other and can, where there is mutual respect, make good each other's defects. We all have both introvert and extravert tendencies; in some the one tendency predominates and in others the other. Professor Eysenck says that in theory each person could be placed on a continuum, one end of which is extreme extraversion, the other end extreme introversion. The great majority of people are somewhat near the middle. Eysenck also links introversion and extraversion to physical constitution. The activity of prayer, regarded as turning to the unseen, will come more easily to the introvert. But genuine prayer is the inspiration of God-oriented action, and this expressing of faith and devotion in practical acts of duty and charity will be easier for the extravert.

The Function Types

Jung further divides both introverts and extraverts according to the four principal ways of dealing with life and its problems;through the senses (that is through seeing, hearing, handling etc.) through thought, through feeling and through intuition. We are all of us in some degree able to exercise each of these functions. Jung classifies individuals according as one or other of them is exercised predominantly. Two of these, sensation and intuition, he calls perceptive functions, because they are concerned with grasping facts. The other two, thinking and feeling, he calls judging functions because they try to evaluate facts; thinking judges statements and opinions as true or false, feeling judges people and things as good or bad, attractive or unattractive. We tend to rely more on one of these ways of coping with our tasks and problems than the others. Our choice results partly from innate constitution, partly from training and early experience. We prefer to play our strong suit.

1 Sensation

If I am an extravert and sensation is my dominant function I shall be interested in things and people as they are. I shall be a realist, a practical man. If I happen to be sensitive to beauty I shall be artistic. If I go to church, whether I am artistic or not, the outward details will be important to me, the way the service is conducted, the other members of the congregation; bricks and mortar will be my concern, church finance will interest me more than doctrine. If I practise private prayer I shall probably find help in set forms of prayer and such adjuncts to prayer as a rosary, crucifix or religious picture. I shall be helped by bodily gestures in prayer, standing with hands raised up or stretched out, kneeling and prostrating myself. I shall readily understand the sacraments which treat me as one of a community and as a bodily being, and address me through sight, hearing, touch and taste. Indeed, corporate worship will mean much more to me than private prayer.

If on the other hand I am an introvert and sensation is my dominant function I shall appreciate religious externals but quite differently from my extravert brother. I shall value them as symbols, as pointers to an unseen world. The sanctuary light will speak of

Christ the true light of all men, vestments will hint at the richness and glory of God, the cloud of incense will speak of prayer and the divine presence. I may be indifferent to the artistic merit of religious pictures, for the pictures will be valued for their power to evoke an inner picture. One reason why the devout often tolerate bad art in their churches is that the pictures and statues are valued for their meaning rather than their beauty. My imagination will probably be important to me. St Teresa of Avila used to picture the scenes and incidents of our Lord's life as happening in her heart. The *Spiritual Exercises* of Saint Ignatius Loyola recommends the use of imagination as a prelude to prayer. For example, you desire to praise and thank God for his incarnation. You imagine the baby Jesus born in Bethlehem, you see in your mind's eye the stable with its occupants, you hear the stable noises, the low murmur of conversation, hushed so as not to wake up the sleeping infant, you may smell the stable smells and even in imagination touch the stable walls and finger the straw. No doubt the picture we paint in the mind's eye will be quite different from what actually happened. But for all our ignorance of the historic details imagination used in this way can bring an element of down-to-earth historic actuality to our worship of the incarnate Christ.

2 Thinking

Let us now consider the kind of person in whom thinking is the dominant function. Where sensation predominates men are concerned with facts, the extravert with facts outside him, the introvert with inner facts or with his inner reaction to external facts. But the thinking type is less concerned with the facts themselves than in thinking about them, analysing them, harmonising them with other facts, forming them into a system. If an extravert he may excel as an administrator, scientist or philosopher; if an introvert his thinking will be subjective and personal; he will want to think out and rationalise his own personal reactions to the problems and tasks of life as he finds it.

Thinking has an important task in safeguarding faith against blind superstition and credulity. A living faith is ever searching for fuller understanding. The thoughtful believer questions received opinions, he is deeply concerned about truth, he desires rationality.

The extravert thinker will try to relate faith to the world in which he lives. He will want to see how it fits in with or challenges the current ideas in science or personal conduct and how it bears on social and international problems. The introvert thinker will be more concerned about doctrine, the truth of the gospel, the godhead of Christ, the nature of the atonement. For the thinker intelligibility in church services will be important; he will want to hear what is said and understand what is done. He will value well-thought-out preaching. Discursive meditation whether on the gospels, on the character of God and his self-revelation in Christ, or on God's presence in the world will be a helpful preparation for prayer. Many of this type would be helped by writing out short prayers based on their reflections and on their understanding of their faith and to use these prayers constantly in private devotion. Meditation on the prayers of the liturgy should help their worship. The Anglican Church caters well on the whole for the thinking type. People of this kind need to resist the temptation to despise emotion and the irrational, for this is just as much part of us as is our capacity to think and needs to find expression in our praying.

3 Feeling

A third function whose predominance helps to differentiate between people is feeling. Like the thinker, the individual of feeling type is concerned to weigh facts up, but unlike him he judges them not as true or false but as good or bad, pleasant or unpleasant. More women than men are of this type. Those of this kind are usually much more competent in human relations than the thinker for we relate to people largely on the level of feeling. Such people may have great intelligence but it will be ruled by feeling. They can be maddening to argue with for they are indifferent to truth and impervious to logic and will change their ground without any sense of shame or inconsistency, But feeling has its own logic. As thinking searches for truth feeling feeds on goodness, it judges value. Feeling is more closely related to the springs of action than thinking is. My reason may convince me that a certain course of action is right but I may do nothing until I feel strongly about it. Feeling also helps prayer more directly than thinking. 'By love may he be gotten and holden but by thought never' writes the author of *The Cloud of*

Unknowing. Those of this type are readily drawn to affective prayer and find it easy and natural to express praise, penitence, gratitude, trust or love. They will appreciate sermons and literature addressed to the heart.

4 *Intuition*

Jung's fourth function is intuition, which he defines as perception by way of the unconscious. The unconscious is the storehouse of past experience which, though apparently forgotten, lives a buried life within, of fleeting impressions quickly forgotten and of telepathic impressions that were never conscious. The man in whom intuition predominates tends to listen to the unconscious, he is like a person standing on the sea shore waiting for what the waves of the unconscious will throw up onto the beach of consciousness. Like the man of sensation type he will be interested in facts, but unlike him he will be concerned not so much about the facts themselves as the possibilities contained in them. It is the facts behind the facts which fascinate him. He is the man of expectation, whether optimistic or gloomy, he relies on flair and hunch, he is a good guesser. When a general was recommended to Napoleon he used to ask, 'Is he lucky?' He was looking for the quality of intuition which enables a general to guess what the enemy is up to. The intuitive knows without being able to say how he knows. Though sometimes mistaken, surprisingly often he is right. If he is an extravert, people and events in the world around him will hold his interest. Politicians and successful business tycoons are usually of this type. The introvert intuitive will be attracted by the spiritual world, the inner world of his own psyche or his inner reactions to the world around him. He may be a man of deep spirituality, a seer or contemplative.

For the extravert intuitive prayer will be closely linked to the service of God in the world. If he is a man of faith he will tend to see prayer as a co-operating with God in the transformation of the world. It will be natural for him to rely on divine guidance in his planning and deciding. Prayer will indeed be for him the inspiration of action. If the extravert intuitive is drawn to the service of God in the world the introvert intuitive is drawn to seek God within himself. He readily sees the truth of what the old spiritual guides affirm, that God is to be found within, in the soul's centre. A contemplative kind of prayer will be normal for him. The so-called darkness of contemplation results from a dim barely perceived awareness of God within, which leaves the conscious mind with the sense of its own ignorance and incapacity. God is obscurely known through certain effects, a strange inner urge and orientation which has been variously described: a waiting on God, a looking towards him, a listening to him, a being still in his presence.

Co-operation and Opposition Between the Functions

Jung was well aware of an immense number of human variables, for example the variations in the ability, intelligence and drive of different individuals, which his theory takes no account of. Further, even within the limits of his analysis each type can be subdivided. A person in whom one function is dominant will commonly rely to a secondary degree on another. Thus a man of sensation type will often rely partly on thinking and a woman of feeling type on intuition.

According to Jung's analysis there is further a fundamental tension not only between the introvert and extravert attitudes but also between some of the functions. In fact each function has its opposite. The two perceptive functions, sensation and intuition, are opposed to each other as are also the two judging functions, thinking and feeling. Feeling interferes with the clear, cool operation of thought and the man who values thinking tends to undervalue and repress feeling. Equally one who habitually judges people and facts by his feelings about them tends to dislike cold, critical reason and repress it. In the same way the man who is interested in the facts under his nose tends to dismiss as idle speculation what may be happening the other side of the hill. Similarly the intuitive interested in possibilities is inclined to be bored with and to overlook the obvious. The more you rely on one function the more of necessity you neglect its opposite. Further, the more you repress a function the more you push it beyond the reach of conscious control and the more violently it may react, just as the harder you throw a rubber ball on the ground the higher it will bounce. A repressed function tends to operate automatically, independently of your intention and will tend to be childish or barbarous in its expression. Thus the thinker can order and direct his thoughts but not his feelings. He can no more control these than he can his dreams; they happen to him and are often violent and disturbing. The woman who is perfectly at home with her feelings and has no problem in deciding what she feels to be best cannot control her thoughts which, often illogical and second hand, happen to her. The temptations which worry us spring as a rule from our repressed and neglected functions. The thinker, for example, may be plagued with violent and irrational dislikes, the spiritual man by temptations of the flesh.

Complications Arising from Early Environmental Influence

What a person is depends partly on inborn temperament and partly on the influence of home and school which may run counter to his nature and aptitudes. For example an infant predisposed by temperament to the introvert attitude might be driven, in order to win the attention and love of a mother who was too reserved in expressing her affection, to develop extravert characteristics. Again another child whom nature designed to be extravert might, in self-defence against a dominating and over-possessive mother, withdraw into his shell and begin to develop some of the typical introvert characteristics. Again at a later stage of growing up a person may be drawn to imitate the style of those whose make-up is different from his own. The personal ideal plays an important part in our development. The small boy commonly aims to become like father, the girl like mother. Relatives and friends of the family may awaken the admiration and influence the ideal of a child, and at school the influence of an admired teacher may be profound. Boys and girls tend to make heroes of some outstanding individual of their own sex, usually a little older than themselves, and take over their hero's style and ideas uncriticised, lock, stock and barrel. This can be a valuable phase in the process of breaking out of the parent dominated world of childhood and moving towards the independence of responsible adulthood. Part of a person's quest to discover his identity is the search to uncover and express outwardly some of his buried personal traits. Many today who are introvert by temperament are forced against their nature to develop extravert characteristics in order to succeed in business. It is common too for those of feeling or intuitive type to be compelled by pressures at school to suppress these characteristics in order to succeed in the educational competition which overvalues rational thinking and the memorising of sheer factual information. These environmental influences must be remembered in trying to understand oneself or anyone else. The changes, sometimes quite dramatic, that occur in middle life can sometimes be understood as the emergence of a person's fundamental nature and the discarding wholly or in part of the attitude built up in response to the pressures of society. Thus Charles de Foncauld the sensualist found himself in middle life by becoming an ascetic and man of prayer.

Prayer for Different Types

To return to the subject of how different kinds of people should pray, it is natural to begin by using your strongest and most developed function. For example, if I am a thinker some kind of reasoned meditation will help me to turn towards God; if feeling is my strong point I should begin with affective prayer. But progress will depend on my enlisting the co-operation of the less developed functions. The inward-looking intuitive will be drawn to some contemplative type of prayer, but if he is to advance spiritually he will need to learn to bring in other functions, such as thinking and feeling, as coadjutors, though not necessarily while praying.

The procedure first of concentrating on the approach a person finds easiest and then trying to develop his weaker side is in line with the way a man normally grows to maturity. In early manhood it is natural to concentrate if possible on what you do well. The demands of career or vocation usually compel a man to forgo interests and pursuits which clash with it. He is usually forced to suppress part of himself in order to make a success of his chosen calling. In youth we have an enormous power of ignoring, of pushing out of mind what conflicts with our immediate concern. As we grow older we have less energy to spare to keep these intrusive interests out. Our energy is increasingly taken up with the business of living, of doing our job, of maintaining our friendships, of caring for our dependents. It becomes of great importance to come to terms with the underdeveloped side of our nature, to broaden our interests and attitudes. I believe that prayer should follow and assist the line of growth to maturity and wholeness and should change its character as we change. We need to be flexible in our method of praying and willing to experiment with new ways. Authentic prayer should spring out of the tensions of actual living.

Problems of Growth to Maturity

To come to terms with the rejected bits of my personality is by no means easy, for the part of myself that I repress takes on the appearance of evil. It seems a standing threat to my deliberately adopted attitude to life. Repressed sensation may give rise to temptations to the crudest licence, repressed feeling to diabolical hates and antagonisms. The person who has refused to use his reason on matters of faith may find himself haunted by doubts about all that he has valued. The practical man who scorns intuition may find himself a prey to fantastic suspicions. This appearance of evil is deceptive. For the part of myself that I reject, though evil in its repressed condition, is potentially good. If you take a perfectly normal dog and chain him up and don't give him enough to eat and deprive him of the exercise and companionship he needs he is likely to become vicious. This is very similar to what happens in repression; the emotions we repress tend to become swollen and unhealthy. The cause of repression is the timidity and narrowness of our conscious attitude to life. To end the repression our attitude must change. But this is not easy. We may find ourselves caught on the horns of a dilemma. It looks as though to give room to the promptings of repressed desires and impulses must mean the abandonment of our standards. On the other hand if we are determined at all costs to keep under these threatening energies we may have to sacrifice almost everything else in order to maintain a strong guard. We are likely to grow narrow and negative. All our energies will be taken up with containing the threat from within. Very likely we shall misunderstand the nature of our problem. For, by the trick of mind called projection, we may easily be convinced that all our troubles are due to hostile forces outside ourselves. We may project our inner troubles on to actual people known to ourselves, or, more likely, on to great collective entities such as communists, capitalists, black people or Jews, and so shut our eyes to their real source.

The most intense efforts will not rescue me from this dilemma, for the harder I try to master the repressed elements within, the more violent will be their reaction. I can escape from it only as I learn to trust myself to the sovereignty of God ruling throughout my being from the soul's centre. This trust in God grows only slowly, but it gradually makes possible the transformation of my conscious attitude so as to make room in it for the things in myself that I have been trying to reject. These feelings and impulses to begin with will seem a threat, gradually they will become something I can live with, finally they will turn into an asset which will bring warmth and energy into all that I do. The experience has been compared to death and rebirth, the death of an old attitude and the coming to birth of a new. We cannot imagine beforehand what the new attitude will be like. The introvert realises that he must learn to face the world around him more positively but does not in the least understand how to do this nor the richer and fuller life that the new attitude will make possible. The extravert is equally at a loss in learning to face his inner being. In either case the change must come about by a process of growth which he can either foster or thwart, but cannot master or control.

Prayer and Spiritual Growth

Prayer ought to take account of and assist the line of growth to maturity. For although maturity is not to be simply identified with holiness, which consists in union with God through obedience to his will, yet the urge to maturity is from God. The work a man is called to do and the burdens he is called to carry may sometimes hinder the growth to maturity, but the more mature a man is the greater will be his capacity to love and serve God and his neighbour. In any case our growth to our full stature can never be complete in this world but must wait its consummation in the world to come.

Since one of the chief obstacles to this growth in our adult years is the obstinate clinging to aims and attitudes that are too narrow and timid, it is important in prayer to disown these aims and acknowledge their inadequacy. This means in practice that I must constantly confess my insufficiency, my inability either to perceive God's will clearly or to do it resolutely; that I have no power of myself to help myself, that without God I can do nothing. This fully traditional type of prayer undermines the resistance of my conscious self to the kind of changes I need to make and helps the growth of the new aims and attitudes which the grace of God is instigating from within. As the little conscious ego makes its act of no confidence in its unaided efforts it opens doors through which Light and Power will flow from within.

Growth to maturity normally proceeds side by side with the growth of self-awareness, which according to one important spiritual tradition is the gateway to a deeper awareness of God. One of the methods of acquiring a fuller self-knowledge, seldom mentioned by spiritual writers, is through recalling and reflecting on your dreams.[3] Dreams are a language of the unconscious. Part of their function is compensatory, to call the attention of the conscious mind to realities which it is neglecting, sometimes in warning, sometimes in encouragement. Dream figures often represent aspects of the dreamer's personality. Bits of myself which I have been neglecting may appear in a dream personified as a tramp or a foreigner who embarrasses me and whom I cannot get rid of. Some knowledge of the interpretation of dream symbols is a help here. But even without this a dream by its atmosphere of gaiety or gloom can help the person who reflects on it to a deeper self-awareness. The images and atmosphere of a dream, if we befriend it and don't let it slip away into oblivion, can help us to approach God more truly as we are.

Further, by the way we pray we can do much to encourage the functions and attitudes that are weak. Imagination may help a great deal here.[4] The introvert before prayer needs to picture in anticipation the situations which will confront him during the coming day and week, and especially the claims of others upon him, and to pray that he may respond to God's will in them. The extravert needs (perhaps by the discipline of regular times of retreat) to develop his power to look within. Similarly I believe it will be of value to make experiment of ways in which to involve our weaker functions in prayer, possibly by experimenting with the prayers or prayer methods of those temperamentally unlike ourselves.

In conclusion I will say something about one practice which can be of great help as a preparation for prayer and as a means of involving ourselves more completely in it by enlisting our undeve-

[3] *Dreams and Nightmares* by J. A. Hadfield, Pelican, gives an account of dreams and then interpretation. Also, in *God, Dreams and Revelation* Morton Kelsey discusses the place of dreams in the spiritual life. Published in USA, Augsburg Publishing House 1974.

[4] For the use of imagination as a help to prayers see *The Other Side of Silence* by Morton Kelsey, SPCK 1977.

loped faculties: *lectio divina*, spiritual reading. Spiritual reading properly done is very unlike typical modern reading in which you race through one book in order to begin another. It is a slow, reflective, prayerful reading with frequent pauses; it is more like meditation than reading a novel; indeed it perhaps ought to be thought of as low-grade meditation. By picturing as best I can the persons and incidents described in what I read I can train my imagination to share in my approach to God. I can train my thinking by reflecting on what I read, by analysing it, perhaps by writing down my reactions to it. I can train feeling, the power to respond sensitively to good and evil, to make discriminating value-judgements, by dwelling on what arouses my feelings even if I sometimes find this painful or embarrassing. I can train intuition by pausing to look beyond the obvious meaning, to look out for hints and nuances, to read and reread obscure passages until they yield up meaning. Often the truth I most need to ponder is initially unattractive, it bores or even repels me. It is important not to hurry over the passages that put us off. Often we can advance only by learning to appreciate what once we despised. Sometimes the way down is the only way to ascend. A useful way of checking the tendency to hurry is to make yourself write a note or comment on what you have read.

Clearly there is something artificial in Jung's analysis of human types, as he would have been the first to admit. We do not fit comfortably into his or any other categories. But I think his system can help us in two ways. First, in understanding people unlike ourselves, that is the majority of people. We learn to understand principally, of course, not by reading books of psychology, whether Jung's or anyone else's but by careful observation and attentive listening and by asking the open-ended questions that encourage people to speak about themselves. Psychology can help us to listen with a keener ear and observe with sharper perceptiveness. The second way it can help us is in our own praying. One of the reasons why our prayer tends to be superficial is that we do not know how to involve the whole of ourselves in it. Our culture tends to exalt the cerebral and repress emotion and the irrational. But this area of our being needs to participate in our approach to God just as much as does our reason. I believe Jung's typology can help to make us more conscious of the neglected potentialities within ourselves, and can enable us to think out ways of bringing these undeveloped powers into our praying.

This study of Jung's types is the revised version of an article published in *New Fire* (Vol I, 1) and was issued as a pamphlet in 1978.